Thoughts from the Mount of Blessing

Original text editon

Ellen G. White

1896

LS Company

ISBN:978-1-0879-8264-9

Copyright©2021

Foreword

Hundreds of thousands of copies of *Thoughts from the Mount of Blessing* have been printed and distributed in nearly a score of languages since it was first published in 1896. In English-reading countries several editions with identical textual content but with variations in format and pagination have been widely distributed. To eliminate confusion in the use of the volume in reference work, a standard page has been adopted which will serve as the basis of present and subsequent printings.

In several former editions, in an endeavor to achieve a certain format, selections from verses of poetry were, with the consent of the author, inserted by the publishers in a number of places throughout the text. In this edition, only poetry selected and made a part of the text by the author herself is retained. The addition of both scripture and subject indexes makes this volume more useful.

That the lessons drawn from the teachings of the master herein set forth may continue to enlighten, encourage, and bless mankind.

Preface

The Sermon on the Mount is Heaven's benediction to the world—a voice from the throne of God.

It was given to mankind to be to them the law of duty and the light of heaven, their hope and consolation in despondency, their joy and comfort in all the vicissitudes and walks of life. Here the Prince of preachers, the Master Teacher, utters the words that the Father gave Him to speak.

The Beatitudes are Christ's greeting, not only to those who believe, but to the whole human family. He seems to have forgotten for a moment that He is in the world, not in heaven; and He uses the familiar salutation of the world of light. Blessings flow from His lips as the gushing forth of a long-sealed current of rich life.

Christ leaves us in no doubt as to the traits of character that He will always recognize and bless. From the ambitious favorites of the world, He turns to those whom they disown, pronouncing all blessed who receive His light and life. To the poor in spirit, the meek, the lowly, the sorrowful, the despised, the persecuted, He opens His arms of refuge, saying, "Come unto Me, ... and I will give you rest."

Christ can look upon the misery of the world without a shade of sorrow for having created man. In the human heart He sees more than sin, more than misery. In His infinite wisdom and love He sees man's possibilities, the height to which he may attain. He knows that, even though human beings have abused their mercies and destroyed their God-given dignity, yet the Creator is to be glorified in their redemption.

Throughout all time the words that Christ spoke from the mount of Beatitudes will retain their power. Every sentence is a jewel from the treasure house of truth. The principles enunciated in this discourse are for all ages and for all classes of men. With divine energy, Christ expressed His faith and hope as He pointed out class after class as blessed because of having formed righteous characters.

Living the life of the Life-giver, through faith in Him, everyone can reach the standard held up in His words.

E.G.W.

Contents

Foreword iii
Preface iv
Chapter 1—On the Mountainside 9
Chapter 2—The Beatitudes 13
    "He opened His mouth, and taught them, saying, Blessed are the poor in spirit: for theirs is the kingdom of heaven."—Matthew 5:2, 3 13
    "Blessed are they that mourn: for they shall be comforted."—Matthew 5:4 15
    "Blessed are the meek."—Matthew 5:5 18
    "Blessed are they which do hunger and thirst after righteousness: for they shall be filled."—Matthew 5:6 .. 21
    "Blessed are the merciful: for they shall obtain mercy."—Matthew 5:7 23
    "Blessed are the pure in heart: for they shall see God."—Matthew 5:8 25
    "Blessed are the peacemakers: for they shall be called the children of God."—Matthew 5:9 27
    "Blessed are they which are persecuted for righteousness' sake: for theirs is the kingdom of heaven."—Matthew 5:10 28
    "Blessed are ye, when men shall revile you."—Matthew 5:11. 30
    "Ye are the salt of the earth."—Matthew 5:13 33
    "Ye are the light of the world."—Matthew 5:14 35
Chapter 3—The Spirituality of the Law 40
    "I am not come to destroy, but to fulfill."—Matthew 5:17 ... 40
    "Whosoever ... shall break one of these least commandments, and shall teach men so, he shall be called the least in the kingdom of heaven."—Matthew 5:19 44
    "Except your righteousness shall exceed the righteousness of the scribes and Pharisees, ye shall in no case enter into the kingdom of heaven."—Matthew 5:20 45

"Everyone who is angry with his brother shall be in danger of the judgment."—Matthew 5:22, R. V. 47
"Be reconciled to thy brother."—Matthew 5:24. 48
"Whosoever looketh on a woman to lust after her hath committed adultery with her already in his heart."—Matthew 5:28. 49
"If thy right hand causeth thee to stumble, cut it off, and cast it from thee."—Matthew 5:30, R. V. 50
"Is it lawful for a man to put away his wife?"—Matthew 19:3. 52
"Swear not at all."—Matthew 5:34. 54
"Resist not him that is evil: but whosoever smiteth thee on thy right cheek, turn to him the other also."—Matthew 5:39, R. V. 56
"Love your enemies."—Matthew 5:44. 59
"Be ye therefore perfect, even as your Father which is in heaven is perfect."—Matthew 5:48. 60
Chapter 4—The True Motive in Service 63
"Take heed that ye do not your righteousness before men, to be seen of them."—Matthew 6:1, margin. 63
"When thou prayest, thou shalt not be as the hypocrites are."—Matthew 6:5. 66
"When ye pray, use not vain repetitions, as the heathen do."—Matthew 6:7. 67
"When ye fast, be not, as the hypocrites."—Matthew 6:16. . 68
"Lay not up for yourselves treasures upon earth."—Matthew 6:19. 69
"If ... thine eye be single, thy whole body shall be full of light."—Matthew 6:22. 71
"No man can serve two masters."—Matthew 6:24. 72
"Be not anxious."—Matthew 6:25, R. V. 74
"Seek ye first the kingdom of God."—Matthew 6:33. 76
"Be not therefore anxious for the morrow.... Sufficient unto the day is the evil thereof."—Matthew 6:34, R. V. 77
Chapter 5—The Lord's Prayer 79
"After this manner therefore pray ye."—Matthew 6:9. 79
"When ye pray, say, Our Father."—Luke 11:2. 80
"Hallowed be Thy name."—Matthew 6:9. 82
"Thy kingdom come."—Matthew 6:10. 83

"Thy will be done in earth, as it is in heaven."—Matthew 6:10. 84
"Give us this day our daily bread."—Matthew 6:11. 84
"Forgive us our sins; for we also forgive everyone that is
    indebted to us."—Luke 11:4. 86
"Bring us not into temptation, but deliver us from the evil
    one."—Matthew 6:13, R. V. 88
"Thine is the kingdom, and the power, and the
    glory."—Matthew 6:13. 91

Chapter 6—Not Judging, but Doing 93
"Judge not, that ye be not judged."—Matthew 7:1. 93
"Why beholdest thou the mote that is in thy brother's
    eye?"—Matthew 7:3. 94
"Give not that which is holy unto the dogs."—Matthew 7:6. . 97
"Ask, and it shall be given you; seek, and ye shall find;
    knock, and it shall be opened unto you."—Matthew 7:7. 98
"Therefore all things whatsoever ye would that men
    should do to you, do ye even so to them."—Matthew
    7:12. 100
"Strait is the gate, and narrow is the way, which leadeth
    unto life."—Matthew 7:14. 103
"Strive to enter in at the strait gate."—Luke 13:24. 105
"Beware of false prophets."—Matthew 7:15. 107
"It fell not; for it was founded upon the rock."—Matthew
    7:25, R. V. 109

Chapter 1—On the Mountainside

More than fourteen centuries before Jesus was born in Bethlehem, the children of Israel gathered in the fair vale of Shechem, and from the mountains on either side the voices of the priests were heard proclaiming the blessings and the curses—"a blessing, if ye obey the commandments of the Lord your God: ... and a curse, if ye will not obey." Deuteronomy 11:27, 28. And thus the mountain from which the words of benediction were spoken came to be known as the mount of blessing. But it was not upon Gerizim that the words were spoken which have come as a benediction to a sinning and sorrowing world. Israel fell short of the high ideal which had been set before her. Another than Joshua must guide His people to the true rest of faith. No longer is Gerizim known as the mount of the Beatitudes, but that unnamed mountain beside the Lake of Gennesaret, where Jesus spoke the words of blessing to His disciples and the multitude.

Let us in imagination go back to that scene, and, as we sit with the disciples on the mountainside, enter into the thoughts and feelings that filled their hearts. Understanding what the words of Jesus meant to those who heard them, we may discern in them a new vividness and beauty, and may also gather for ourselves their deeper lessons.

When the Saviour began His ministry, the popular conception of the Messiah and His work was such as wholly unfitted the people to receive Him. The spirit of true devotion had been lost in tradition and ceremonialism, and the prophecies were interpreted at the dictate of proud, world-loving hearts. The Jews looked for the coming One, not as a Saviour from sin, but as a great prince who should bring all nations under the supremacy of the Lion of the tribe of Judah. In vain had John the Baptist, with the heart-searching power of the ancient prophets, called them to repentance. In vain had he, beside the Jordan, pointed to Jesus as the Lamb of God, that taketh away the sin of the world. God was seeking to direct their minds to Isaiah's prophecy of the suffering Saviour, but they would not hear.

Had the teachers and leaders in Israel yielded to His transforming grace, Jesus would have made them His ambassadors among men. In Judea first the coming of the kingdom had been proclaimed, and the call to repentance had been given. In the act of driving out the desecrators from the temple at Jerusalem, Jesus had announced Himself as the Messiah—the One who should cleanse the soul from the defilement of sin and make His people a holy temple unto the Lord. But the Jewish leaders would not humble themselves to receive the lowly Teacher from Nazareth. At His second visit to Jerusalem He was arraigned before the Sanhedrin, and fear of the people alone prevented these dignitaries from trying to take His life. Then it was that, leaving Judea, He entered upon His ministry in Galilee.

His work there had continued some months before the Sermon on the Mount was given. The message He had proclaimed throughout the land, "The kingdom of heaven is at hand" (Matthew 4:17), had arrested the attention of all classes, and had still further fanned the flame of their ambitious hopes. The fame of the new Teacher had spread beyond the limits of Palestine, and, notwithstanding the attitude of the hierarchy, the feeling was widespread that this might be the hoped-for Deliverer. Great multitudes thronged the steps of Jesus, and the popular enthusiasm ran high.

The time had come for the disciples who had been most closely associated with Christ to unite more directly in His work, that these vast throngs might not be left uncared for, as sheep without a shepherd. Some of these disciples had joined themselves to Him at the beginning of His ministry, and nearly all the twelve had been associated together as members of the family of Jesus. Yet they also, misled by the teaching of the rabbis, shared the popular expectation of an earthly kingdom. They could not comprehend the movements of Jesus. Already they had been perplexed and troubled that He made no effort to strengthen His cause by securing the support of the priests and rabbis, that He did nothing to establish His authority as an earthly king. A great work was yet to be accomplished for these disciples before they would be prepared for the sacred trust that would be theirs when Jesus should ascend to heaven. Yet they had responded to the love of Christ, and, though slow of heart to believe, Jesus saw in them those whom He could train and discipline for His great work. And now that they had been long enough with

Him to establish, in a measure, their faith in the divine character of His mission, and the people also had received evidence of His power which they could not question, the way was prepared for an avowal of the principles of His kingdom that would help them to comprehend its true nature.

Alone upon a mountain near the Sea of Galilee, Jesus had spent all night in prayer for these chosen ones. At the dawn He called them to Him, and, with words of prayer and instruction, laid His hands upon their heads in benediction, setting them apart to the gospel work. Then He repaired with them to the seaside, where in the early morning a great multitude had already begun to assemble.

Besides the usual crowd from the Galilean towns, there were great numbers from Judea, and from Jerusalem itself; from Perea, and from the half-heathen population of Decapolis; from Idumea, away to the south of Judea, and from Tyre and Sidon, the Phoenician cities on the shore of the Mediterranean. "Hearing what great things He did," they "came to hear Him, and to be healed of their diseases; and ... power came forth from Him, and healed them all." Mark 3:8 , R.V.; Luke 6:17-19 , R.V.

Then, as the narrow beach did not afford even standing room within reach of His voice for all who desired to hear Him, Jesus led the way back to the mountainside. Reaching a level space that afforded a pleasant gathering place for the vast assembly, He seated Himself upon the grass, and His disciples and the multitude followed His example.

With a feeling that something more than usual might be expected, the disciples had pressed about their Master. From the events of the morning they gathered assurance that some announcement was about to be made in regard to the kingdom which, as they fondly hoped, He was soon to establish. A feeling of expectancy pervaded the multitude also, and eager faces gave evidence of the deep interest.

As they sat upon the green hillside, awaiting the words of the divine Teacher, their hearts were filled with thoughts of future glory. There were scribes and Pharisees who looked forward to the day when they should have dominion over the hated Romans and possess the riches and splendor of the world's great empire. The poor peasants and fishermen hoped to hear the assurance that their wretched hovels, the scanty food, the life of toil, and fear of want, were to be exchanged for mansions of plenty and days of ease. In place of the one coarse garment which was their covering by day and their blanket at night, they hoped that Christ would give them the rich and costly robes of their conquerors.

All hearts thrilled with the proud hope that Israel was soon to be honored before the nations as the chosen of the Lord, and Jerusalem exalted as the head of a universal kingdom.

Chapter 2—The Beatitudes

"He opened His mouth, and taught them, saying, Blessed are the poor in spirit: for theirs is the kingdom of heaven."—Matthew 5:2, 3.

As something strange and new, these words fall upon the ears of the wondering multitude. Such teaching is contrary to all they have ever heard from priest or rabbi. They see in it nothing to flatter their pride or to feed their ambitious hopes. But there is about this new Teacher a power that holds them spellbound. The sweetness of divine love flows from His very presence as the fragrance from a flower. His words fall like "rain upon the mown grass: as showers that water the earth." Psalm 72:6. All feel instinctively that here is One who reads the secrets of the soul, yet who comes near to them with tender compassion. Their hearts open to Him, and, as they listen, the Holy Spirit unfolds to them something of the meaning of that lesson which humanity in all ages so needs to learn.

In the days of Christ the religious leaders of the people felt that they were rich in spiritual treasure. The prayer of the Pharisee, "God, I thank Thee, that I am not as the rest of men" (Luke 18:11, R.V.), expressed the feeling of his class and, to a great degree, of the whole nation. But in the throng that surrounded Jesus there were some who had a sense of their spiritual poverty. When in the miraculous draft of fishes the divine power of Christ was revealed, Peter fell at the Saviour's feet, exclaiming, "Depart from me; for I am a sinful man, O Lord" (Luke 5:8); so in the multitude gathered upon the mount there were souls who, in the presence of His purity, felt that they were "wretched, and miserable, and poor, and blind, and naked" (Revelation 3:17); and they longed for "the grace of God that bringeth salvation" (Titus 2:11). In these souls, Christ's words of greeting awakened hope; they saw that their lives were under the benediction of God.

Jesus had presented the cup of blessing to those who felt that they were "rich, and increased with goods" (Revelation 3:17), and had need of nothing, and they had turned with scorn from the gracious gift. He who feels whole, who thinks that he is reasonably good, and is contented with his condition, does not seek to become a partaker of the grace and righteousness of Christ. Pride feels no need, and so it closes the heart against Christ and the infinite blessings He came to give. There is no room for Jesus in the heart of such a person. Those who are rich and honorable in their own eyes do not ask in faith, and receive the blessing of God. They feel that they are full, therefore they go away empty. Those who know that they cannot possibly save themselves, or of themselves do any righteous action, are the ones who appreciate the help that Christ can bestow. They are the poor in spirit, whom He declares to be blessed.

[8] Whom Christ pardons, He first makes penitent, and it is the office of the Holy Spirit to convince of sin. Those whose hearts have been moved by the convicting Spirit of God see that there is nothing good in themselves. They see that all they have ever done is mingled with self and sin. Like the poor publican, they stand afar off, not daring to lift up so much as their eyes to heaven, and cry, "God, be merciful to me the sinner." Luke 18:13, R.V., margin. And they are blessed. There is forgiveness for the penitent; for Christ is "the Lamb of God, which taketh away the sin of the world." John 1:29. God's promise is: "Though your sins be as scarlet, they shall be as white as snow; though they be red like crimson, they shall be as wool."" A new heart also will I give you.... And I will put My Spirit within you." Isaiah 1:18; Ezekiel 36:26, 27.

Of the poor in spirit Jesus says, "Theirs is the kingdom of heaven." This kingdom is not, as Christ's hearers had hoped, a temporal and earthly dominion. Christ was opening to men the spiritual kingdom of His love, His grace, His righteousness. The ensign of the Messiah's reign is distinguished by the likeness of the Son of man. His subjects are the poor in spirit, the meek, the persecuted for righteousness' sake. The kingdom of heaven is theirs. Though not yet fully accomplished, the work is begun in them which will make them "meet to be partakers of the inheritance of the saints in light." Colossians 1:12.

All who have a sense of their deep soul poverty, who feel that they have nothing good in themselves, may find righteousness and strength by looking unto Jesus. He says, "Come unto Me, all ye that labor and are heavy-laden." Matthew 11:28. He bids you exchange your poverty for the riches of His grace. We are not worthy of God's love, but Christ, our surety, is worthy, and is abundantly able to save all who shall come unto Him. Whatever may have been your past experience, however discouraging your present circumstances, if you will come to Jesus just as you are, weak, helpless, and despairing, our compassionate Saviour will meet you a great way off, and will throw about you His arms of love and His robe of righteousness. He presents us to the Father clothed in the white raiment of His own character. He pleads before God in our behalf, saying: I have taken the sinner's place. Look not upon this wayward child, but look on Me. Does Satan plead loudly against our souls, accusing of sin, and claiming us as his prey, the blood of Christ pleads with greater power.

"Surely, shall one say, in the Lord have I righteousness and strength.... In the Lord shall all the seed of Israel be justified, and shall glory." Isaiah 45:24, 25.

"Blessed are they that mourn: for they shall be comforted."—Matthew 5:4.

The mourning here brought to view is true heart sorrow for sin. Jesus says, "I, if I be lifted up from the earth, will draw all men unto Me." John 12:32. And as one is drawn to behold Jesus uplifted on the cross, he discerns the sinfulness of humanity. He sees that it is sin which scourged and crucified the Lord of glory. He sees that, while he has been loved with unspeakable tenderness, his life has been a continual scene of ingratitude and rebellion. He has forsaken his best Friend and abused heaven's most precious gift. He has crucified to himself the Son of God afresh and pierced anew that bleeding and stricken heart. He is separated from God by a gulf of sin that is broad and black and deep, and he mourns in brokenness of heart.

Such mourning "shall be comforted." God reveals to us our guilt that we may flee to Christ, and through Him be set free from the bondage of sin, and rejoice in the liberty of the sons of God. In true contrition we may come to the foot of the cross, and there leave our burdens.

The Saviour's words have a message of comfort to those also who are suffering affliction or bereavement. Our sorrows do not spring out of the ground. God "doth not afflict willingly nor grieve the children of men." Lamentations 3:33. When He permits trials and afflictions, it is "for our profit, that we might be partakers of His holiness." Hebrews 12:10. If received in faith, the trial that seems so bitter and hard to bear will prove a blessing. The cruel blow that blights the joys of earth will be the means of turning our eyes to heaven. How many there are who would never have known Jesus had not sorrow led them to seek comfort in Him!

The trials of life are God's workmen, to remove the impurities and roughness from our character. Their hewing, squaring, and chiseling, their burnishing and polishing, is a painful process; it is hard to be pressed down to the grinding wheel. But the stone is brought forth prepared to fill its place in the heavenly temple. Upon no useless material does the Master bestow such careful, thorough work. Only His precious stones are polished after the similitude of a palace.

The Lord will work for all who put their trust in Him. Precious victories will be gained by the faithful. Precious lessons will be learned. Precious experiences will be realized.

Our heavenly Father is never unmindful of those whom sorrow has touched. When David went up the Mount Olivet, "and wept as he went up, and had his head covered, and he went barefoot" (2 Samuel 15:30), the Lord was looking pityingly upon him. David was clothed in sackcloth, and his conscience was scourging him. The outward signs of humiliation testified of his contrition. In tearful, heartbroken utterances he presented his case to God, and the Lord did not forsake His servant. Never was David dearer to the heart of Infinite Love than when, conscience-smitten, he fled for his life from his enemies, who had been stirred to rebellion by his own son. The Lord says, "As many as I love, I rebuke and chasten: be zealous therefore, and repent." Revelation 3:19. Christ lifts up the contrite heart and refines the mourning soul until it becomes His abode.

But when tribulation comes upon us, how many of us are like Jacob! We think it the hand of an enemy; and in the darkness we wrestle blindly until our strength is spent, and we find no comfort or deliverance. To Jacob the divine touch at break of day revealed the One with whom he had been contending—the Angel of the covenant; and, weeping and helpless, he fell upon the breast of Infinite Love, to receive the blessing for which his soul longed. We also need to learn that trials mean benefit, and not to despise the chastening of the Lord nor faint when we are rebuked of Him.

"Happy is the man whom God correcteth: ... He maketh sore, and bindeth up: He woundeth, and His hands make whole. He shall deliver thee in six troubles: yea, in seven there shall no evil touch thee." Job 5:17-19. To every stricken one, Jesus comes with the ministry of healing. The life of bereavement, pain, and suffering may be brightened by precious revealings of His presence. [12]

God would not have us remain pressed down by dumb sorrow, with sore and breaking hearts. He would have us look up and behold His dear face of love. The blessed Saviour stands by many whose eyes are so blinded by tears that they do not discern Him. He longs to clasp our hands, to have us look to Him in simple faith, permitting Him to guide us. His heart is open to our griefs, our sorrows, and our trials. He has loved us with an everlasting love and with loving-kindness compassed us about. We may keep the heart stayed upon Him and meditate upon His loving-kindness all the day. He will lift the soul above the daily sorrow and perplexity, into a realm of peace.

Think of this, children of suffering and sorrow, and rejoice in hope. "This is the victory that overcometh the world, even our faith." 1 John 5:4.

Blessed are they also who weep with Jesus in sympathy with the world's sorrow and in sorrow for its sin. In such mourning there is intermingled no thought of self. Jesus was the Man of Sorrows, enduring heart anguish such as no language can portray. His spirit was torn and bruised by the transgressions of men. He toiled with self-consuming zeal to relieve the wants and woes of humanity, and His heart was heavy with sorrow as He saw multitudes refuse to come to Him that they might have life. All who are followers of Christ will share in this experience. As they partake of His love they will enter into His travail for the saving of the lost. They share in the sufferings of Christ, and they will share also in the glory that shall [13] be revealed. One with Him in His work, drinking with Him the cup of sorrow, they are partakers also of His joy.

It was through suffering that Jesus obtained the ministry of consolation. In all the affliction of humanity He is afflicted; and "in that He Himself hath suffered being tempted, He is able to succor them that are tempted." Isaiah 63:9; Hebrews 2:18. In this ministry every soul that has entered into the fellowship of His sufferings is privileged to share. "As the sufferings of Christ abound in us, so our consolation also aboundeth by Christ." 2 Corinthians 1:5. The Lord has special grace for the mourner, and its power is to melt hearts, to win souls. His love opens a channel into the wounded and bruised soul, and becomes a healing balsam to those who sorrow. "The Father of mercies, and the God of all comfort ... comforteth us in all our tribulation, that we may be able to comfort them which are in any trouble, by the comfort wherewith we ourselves are comforted of God." 2 Corinthians 1:3, 4.

"Blessed are the meek."—Matthew 5:5.

Throughout the Beatitudes there is an advancing line of Christian experience. Those who have felt their need of Christ, those who have mourned because of sin and have sat with Christ in the school of affliction, will learn meekness from the divine Teacher.

Patience and gentleness under wrong were not characteristics prized by the heathen or by the Jews. The statement made by Moses under the inspiration of the Holy Spirit, that he was the meekest man upon the earth, would not have been regarded by the people of his time as a commendation; it would rather have excited pity or contempt. But Jesus places meekness among the first qualifications for His kingdom. In His own life and character the divine beauty of this precious grace is revealed.

Jesus, the brightness of the Father's glory, thought "it not a thing to be grasped to be on an equality with God, but emptied Himself, taking the form of a servant." Philippians 2:6, 7 , R.V., margin. Through all the lowly experiences of life He consented to pass, walking among the children of men, not as a king, to demand homage, but as one whose mission it was to serve others. There was in His manner no taint of bigotry, no cold austerity. The world's

Redeemer had a greater than angelic nature, yet united with His divine majesty were meekness and humility that attracted all to Himself.

Jesus emptied Himself, and in all that He did, self did not appear. He subordinated all things to the will of His Father. When His mission on earth was about to close, He could say, "I have glorified Thee on the earth: I have finished the work which Thou gavest Me to do." John 17:4. And He bids us, "Learn of Me; for I am meek and lowly in heart." "If any man will come after Me, let him deny himself" (Matthew 11:29; 16:24); let self be dethroned and no longer hold the supremacy of the soul.

He who beholds Christ in His self-denial, His lowliness of heart, will be constrained to say, as did Daniel, when he beheld One like the sons of men, "My comeliness was turned in me into corruption." Daniel 10:8. The independence and self-supremacy in which we glory are seen in their true vileness as tokens of servitude to Satan. Human nature is ever struggling for expression, ready for contest; but he who learns of Christ is emptied of self, of pride, of love of supremacy, and there is silence in the soul. Self is yielded to the disposal of the Holy Spirit. Then we are not anxious to have the highest place. We have no ambition to crowd and elbow ourselves into notice; but we feel that our highest place is at the feet of our Saviour. We look to Jesus, waiting for His hand to lead, listening for His voice to guide. The apostle Paul had this experience, and he said, "I am crucified with Christ: nevertheless I live; yet not I, but Christ liveth in me: and the life which I now live in the flesh I live by the faith of the Son of God, who loved me, and gave Himself for me." Galatians 2:20.

When we receive Christ as an abiding guest in the soul, the peace of God, which passeth all understanding, will keep our hearts and minds through Christ Jesus. The Saviour's life on earth, though lived in the midst of conflict, was a life of peace. While angry enemies were constantly pursuing Him, He said, "He that sent Me is with Me: the Father hath not left Me alone; for I do always those things that please Him." John 8:29. No storm of human or satanic wrath could disturb the calm of that perfect communion with God. And He says to us, "Peace I leave with you, My peace I give unto you." "Take My yoke upon you, and learn of Me; for I am meek and lowly in heart: and ye shall find rest." John 14:27; Matthew 11:29. Bear with Me the yoke of service for the glory of God and the uplifting of humanity, and you will find the yoke easy and the burden light.

It is the love of self that destroys our peace. While self is all alive, we stand ready continually to guard it from mortification and insult; but when we are dead, and our life is hid with Christ in God, we shall not take neglects or slights to heart. We shall be deaf to reproach and blind to scorn and insult. "Love suffereth long, and is kind; love envieth not; love vaunteth not itself, is not puffed up, doth not behave itself unseemly, seeketh not its own, is not provoked, taketh not account of evil; rejoiceth not in unrighteousness, but rejoiceth with the truth; beareth all things, believeth all things, hopeth all things, endureth all things. Love never faileth." 1 Corinthians 13:4-8, R.V.

Happiness drawn from earthly sources is as changeable as varying circumstances can make it; but the peace of Christ is a constant and abiding peace. It does not depend upon any circumstances in life, on the amount of worldly goods or the number of earthly friends. Christ is the fountain of living water, and happiness drawn from Him can never fail.

The meekness of Christ, manifested in the home, will make the inmates happy; it provokes no quarrel, gives back no angry answer, but soothes the irritated temper and diffuses a gentleness that is felt by all within its charmed circle. Wherever cherished, it makes the families of earth a part of the one great family above.

Far better would it be for us to suffer under false accusation than to inflict upon ourselves the torture of retaliation upon our enemies. The spirit of hatred and revenge originated with Satan, and can bring only evil to him who cherishes it. Lowliness of heart, that meekness which is the fruit of abiding in Christ, is the true secret of blessing. "He will beautify the meek with salvation." Psalm 149:4.

The meek "shall inherit the earth." It was through the desire for self-exaltation that sin entered into the world, and our first parents lost the dominion over this fair earth, their kingdom. It is through self-abnegation that Christ redeems what was lost. And He says we are to overcome as He did. Revelation 3:21. Through humility and self-surrender we may become heirs with Him when "the meek shall inherit the earth." Psalm 37:11.

The earth promised to the meek will not be like this, darkened with the shadow of death and the curse. "We, according to His promise, look for new heavens and a new earth, wherein dwelleth righteousness." "There shall be no more curse: but the throne of God and of the Lamb shall be in it; and His servants shall serve Him." 2 Peter 3:13; Revelation 22:3.

There is no disappointment, no sorrow, no sin, no one who shall say, I am sick; there are no burial trains, no mourning, no death, no partings, no broken hearts; but Jesus is there, peace is there. There "they shall not hunger nor thirst; neither shall the heat nor sun smite them: for He that hath mercy on them shall lead them, even by the springs of water shall He guide them." Isaiah 49:10.

"Blessed are they which do hunger and thirst after righteousness: for they shall be filled."—Matthew 5:6.

Righteousness is holiness, likeness to God, and "God is love." 1 John 4:16. It is conformity to the law of God, for "all Thy commandments are righteousness" (Psalm 119:172), and "love is the fulfilling of the law" (Romans 13:10). Righteousness is love, and love is the light and the life of God. The righteousness of God is embodied in Christ. We receive righteousness by receiving Him.

Not by painful struggles or wearisome toil, not by gift or sacrifice, is righteousness obtained; but it is freely given to every soul who hungers and thirsts to receive it. "Ho, every one that thirsteth, come ye to the waters, and he that hath no money; come ye, buy, and eat, ... without money and without price." "Their righteousness is of Me, saith the Lord," and, "This is His name whereby He shall be called, The Lord Our Righteousness." Isaiah 55:1; 54:17; Jeremiah 23:6.

No human agent can supply that which will satisfy the hunger and thirst of the soul. But Jesus says, "Behold, I stand at the door, and knock: if any man hear My voice, and open the door, I will come in to him, and will sup with him, and he with Me." "I am the bread of life: he that cometh to Me shall never hunger; and he that believeth on Me shall never thirst." Revelation 3:20; John 6:35.

As we need food to sustain our physical strength, so do we need Christ, the Bread from heaven, to sustain spiritual life and impart strength to work the works of God. As the body is continually receiving the nourishment that sustains life and vigor, so the soul must be constantly communing with Christ, submitting to Him and depending wholly upon Him.

As the weary traveler seeks the spring in the desert and, finding it, quenches his burning thirst, so will the Christian thirst for and obtain the pure water of life, of which Christ is the fountain.

As we discern the perfection of our Saviour's character we shall desire to become wholly transformed and renewed in the image of His purity. The more we know of God, the higher will be our ideal of character and the more earnest our longing to reflect His likeness. A divine element combines with the human when the soul reaches out after God and the longing heart can say, "My soul, wait thou only upon God; for my expectation is from Him." Psalm 62:5.

If you have a sense of need in your soul, if you hunger and thirst after righteousness, this is an evidence that Christ has wrought upon your heart, in order that He may be sought unto to do for you, through the endowment of the Holy Spirit, those things which it is impossible for you to do for yourself. We need not seek to quench our thirst at shallow streams; for the great fountain is just above us, of whose abundant waters we may freely drink, if we will rise a little higher in the pathway of faith.

[20]

The words of God are the wellsprings of life. As you seek unto those living springs you will, through the Holy Spirit, be brought into communion with Christ. Familiar truths will present themselves to your mind in a new aspect, texts of Scripture will burst upon you with a new meaning as a flash of light, you will see the relation of other truths to the work of redemption, and you will know that Christ is leading you, a divine Teacher is at your side.

Jesus said, "The water that I shall give him shall be in him a well of water springing up into everlasting life." John 4:14. As the Holy Spirit opens to you the truth you will treasure up the most precious experiences and will long to speak to others of the comforting things that have been revealed to you. When brought into association with them you will communicate some fresh thought in regard to the character or the work of Christ. You will have some fresh revelation of His pitying love to impart to those who love Him and to those who love Him not.

"Give, and it shall be given unto you" (Luke 6:38); for the word of God is "a fountain of gardens, a well of living waters, and streams of Lebanon" (Song of Solomon 4:15). The heart that has once tasted the love of Christ, cries out continually for a deeper draft, and as you impart you will receive in richer and more abundant measure. Every revelation of God to the soul increases the capacity to know and to love. The continual cry of the heart is, "More of Thee," and ever the Spirit's answer is, "Much more." Romans 5:9, 10. For our God delights to do "exceeding abundantly above all that we ask or think." Ephesians 3:20. To Jesus, who emptied Himself for the salvation of lost humanity, the Holy Spirit was given without measure. So it will be given to every follower of Christ when the whole heart is surrendered for His indwelling. Our Lord Himself has given the command, "Be filled with the Spirit" (Ephesians 5:18), and this command is also a promise of its fulfillment. It was the good pleasure of the Father that in Christ should "all the fullness dwell," and "in Him ye are made full." Colossians 1:19 , R.V.; 2:10, R.V.

God has poured out His love unstintedly, as the showers that refresh the earth. He says, "Let the skies pour down righteousness: let the earth open, and let them bring forth salvation, and let righteousness spring up together." "When the poor and needy seek water, and there is none, and their tongue faileth for thirst, I the Lord will hear them, I the God of Israel will not forsake them. I will open rivers in high places, and fountains in the midst of the valleys: I will make the wilderness a pool of water, and the dry land springs of water." Isaiah 45:8; 41:17, 18.

"Of His fullness have all we received, and grace for grace." John 1:16.

"Blessed are the merciful: for they shall obtain mercy."—Matthew 5:7.

The heart of man is by nature cold and dark and unloving; whenever one manifests a spirit of mercy and forgiveness, he does it not of himself, but through the influence of the divine Spirit moving upon his heart. "We love, because He first loved us." 1 John 4:19 , R.V.

God is Himself the source of all mercy. His name is "merciful and gracious." Exodus 34:6. He does not treat us according to our desert. He does not ask if we are worthy of His love, but He pours upon us the riches of His love, to make us worthy. He is not vindictive. He seeks not to punish, but to redeem. Even the severity which He manifests through His providences is manifested for the salvation of the wayward. He yearns with intense desire to relieve the woes of men and to apply His balsam to their wounds. It is true that God "will by no means clear the guilty" (Exodus 34:7), but He would take away the guilt.

The merciful are "partakers of the divine nature," and in them the compassionate love of God finds expression. All whose hearts are in sympathy with the heart of Infinite Love will seek to reclaim and not to condemn. Christ dwelling in the soul is a spring that never runs dry. Where He abides, there will be an overflowing of beneficence.

To the appeal of the erring, the tempted, the wretched victims of want and sin, the Christian does not ask, Are they worthy? but, How can I benefit them? In the most wretched, the most debased, he sees souls whom Christ died to save and for whom God has given to His children the ministry of reconciliation.

The merciful are those who manifest compassion to the poor, the suffering, and the oppressed. Job declares, "I delivered the poor that cried, and the fatherless, and him that had none to help him. The blessing of him that was ready to perish came upon me: and I caused the widow's heart to sing for joy. I put on righteousness, and it clothed me: my judgment was as a robe and a diadem. I was eyes to the blind, and feet was I to the lame. I was a father to the poor: and the cause which I knew not I searched out." Job 29:12-16.

There are many to whom life is a painful struggle; they feel their deficiencies and are miserable and unbelieving; they think they have nothing for which to be grateful. Kind words, looks of sympathy, expressions of appreciation, would be to many a struggling and lonely one as the cup of cold water to a thirsty soul. A word of sympathy, an act of kindness, would lift burdens that rest heavily upon weary shoulders. And every word or deed of unselfish kindness is an expression of the love of Christ for lost humanity.

The merciful "shall obtain mercy." "The soul of blessing shall be made fat: and he that watereth shall be watered also himself."

Proverbs 11:25 , margin. There is sweet peace for the compassionate spirit, a blessed satisfaction in the life of self-forgetful service for the good of others. The Holy Spirit that abides in the soul and is manifest in the life will soften hard hearts and awaken sympathy and tenderness. You will reap that which you sow. "Blessed is he that considereth the poor.... The Lord will preserve him, and keep him alive; and he shall be blessed upon the earth: and Thou wilt not deliver him unto the will of his enemies. The Lord will strengthen him upon the bed of languishing: Thou wilt make all his bed in his sickness." Psalm 41:1-3.

He who has given his life to God in ministry to His children is linked with Him who has all the resources of the universe at His command. His life is bound up by the golden chain of the immutable promises with the life of God. The Lord will not fail him in the hour of suffering and need. "My God shall supply all your need according to His riches in glory by Christ Jesus." Philippians 4:19. And in the hour of final need the merciful shall find refuge in the mercy of the compassionate Saviour and shall be received into everlasting habitations.

"Blessed are the pure in heart: for they shall see God."—Matthew 5:8.

The Jews were so exacting in regard to ceremonial purity that their regulations were extremely burdensome. Their minds were occupied with rules and restrictions and the fear of outward defilement, and they did not perceive the stain that selfishness and malice impart to the soul.

Jesus does not mention this ceremonial purity as one of the conditions of entering into His kingdom, but points out the need of purity of heart. The wisdom that is from above "is first pure." James 3:17. Into the city of God there will enter nothing that defiles. All who are to be dwellers there will here have become pure in heart. In one who is learning of Jesus, there will be manifest a growing distaste for careless manners, unseemly language, and coarse thought. When Christ abides in the heart, there will be purity and refinement of thought and manner.

But the words of Jesus, "Blessed are the pure in heart," have a deeper meaning—not merely pure in the sense in which the world understands purity, free from that which is sensual, pure from lust, but true in the hidden purposes and motives of the soul, free from pride and self-seeking, humble, unselfish, childlike.

Only like can appreciate like. Unless you accept in your own life the principle of self-sacrificing love, which is the principle of His character, you cannot know God. The heart that is deceived by Satan, looks upon God as a tyrannical, relentless being; the selfish characteristics of humanity, even of Satan himself, are attributed to the loving Creator. "Thou thoughtest," He says, "that I was altogether such an one as thyself." Psalm 50:21. His providences are interpreted as the expression of an arbitrary, vindictive nature. So with the Bible, the treasure house of the riches of His grace. The glory of its truths, that are as high as heaven and compass eternity, is undiscerned. To the great mass of mankind, Christ Himself is "as a root out of a dry ground," and they see in Him "no beauty that" they "should desire Him." Isaiah 53:2. When Jesus was among men, the revelation of God in humanity, the scribes and Pharisees declared to Him, "Thou art a Samaritan, and hast a devil." John 8:48. Even His disciples were so blinded by the selfishness of their hearts that they were slow to understand Him who had come to manifest to them the Father's love. This was why Jesus walked in solitude in the midst of men. He was understood fully in heaven alone.

When Christ shall come in His glory, the wicked cannot endure to behold Him. The light of His presence, which is life to those who love Him, is death to the ungodly. The expectation of His coming is to them a "fearful looking for of judgment and fiery indignation." Hebrews 10:27. When He shall appear, they will pray to be hidden from the face of Him who died to redeem them.

But to hearts that have become purified through the indwelling of the Holy Spirit, all is changed. These can know God. Moses was hid in the cleft of the rock when the glory of the Lord was revealed to him; and it is when we are hid in Christ that we behold the love of God.

"He that loveth pureness of heart, for the grace of his lips the King shall be his friend." Proverbs 22:11. By faith we behold Him here and now. In our daily experience we discern His goodness and compassion in the manifestation of His providence. We recognize Him in the character of His Son. The Holy Spirit takes the truth concerning God and Him whom He hath sent, and opens it to the understanding and to the heart. The pure in heart see God in a new and endearing relation, as their Redeemer; and while they discern the purity and loveliness of His character, they long to reflect His image. They see Him as a Father longing to embrace a repenting son, and their hearts are filled with joy unspeakable and full of glory.

The pure in heart discern the Creator in the works of His mighty hand, in the things of beauty that comprise the universe. In His written word they read in clearer lines the revelation of His mercy, His goodness, and His grace. The truths that are hidden from the wise and prudent are revealed to babes. The beauty and preciousness of truth, which are undiscerned by the worldly-wise, are constantly unfolding to those who have a trusting, childlike desire to know and to do the will of God. We discern the truth by becoming, ourselves, partakers of the divine nature.

The pure in heart live as in the visible presence of God during the time He apportions them in this world. And they will also see Him face to face in the future, immortal state, as did Adam when he walked and talked with God in Eden. "Now we see through a glass, darkly; but then face to face." 1 Corinthians 13:12.

"Blessed are the peacemakers: for they shall be called the children of God."—Matthew 5:9.

Christ is "the Prince of Peace" (Isaiah 9:6), and it is His mission to restore to earth and heaven the peace that sin has broken. "Being justified by faith, we have peace with God through our Lord Jesus Christ." Romans 5:1. Whoever consents to renounce sin and open his heart to the love of Christ, becomes a partaker of this heavenly peace.

There is no other ground of peace than this. The grace of Christ received into the heart, subdues enmity; it allays strife and fills the soul with love. He who is at peace with God and his fellow men cannot be made miserable. Envy will not be in his heart; evil surmisings will find no room there; hatred cannot exist. The heart that is in harmony with God is a partaker of the peace of heaven and will diffuse its blessed influence on all around. The spirit of peace will rest like dew upon hearts weary and troubled with worldly strife.

Christ's followers are sent to the world with the message of peace. Whoever, by the quiet, unconscious influence of a holy life, shall reveal the love of Christ; whoever, by word or deed, shall lead another to renounce sin and yield his heart to God, is a peacemaker.

And "blessed are the peacemakers: for they shall be called the children of God." The spirit of peace is evidence of their connection with heaven. The sweet savor of Christ surrounds them. The fragrance of the life, the loveliness of the character, reveal to the world the fact that they are children of God. Men take knowledge of them that they have been with Jesus. "Everyone that loveth is born of God." "If any man have not the Spirit of Christ, he is none of His;" but "as many as are led by the Spirit of God, they are the sons of God." 1 John 4:7; Romans 8:9, 14.

"And the remnant of Jacob shall be in the midst of many people as a dew from the Lord, as the showers upon the grass, that tarrieth not for man, nor waiteth for the sons of men." Micah 5:7.

[29] "Blessed are they which are persecuted for righteousness' sake: for theirs is the kingdom of heaven."—Matthew 5:10.

Jesus does not present to His followers the hope of attaining earthly glory and riches, and of having a life free from trial, but He presents to them the privilege of walking with their Master in the paths of self-denial and reproach, because the world knows them not.

He who came to redeem the lost world was opposed by the united forces of the adversaries of God and man. In an unpitying confederacy, evil men and evil angels arrayed themselves against the Prince of Peace. Though His every word and act breathed of divine compassion, His unlikeness to the world provoked the bitterest hostility. Because He would give no license for the exercise of the evil passions of our nature, He aroused the fiercest opposition and enmity. So it is with all who will live godly in Christ Jesus. Between righteousness and sin, love and hatred, truth and falsehood, there is an irrepressible conflict. When one presents the love of Christ and the beauty of holiness, he is drawing away the subjects of Satan's kingdom, and the prince of evil is aroused to resist it. Persecution and reproach await all who are imbued with the Spirit of Christ. The character of the persecution changes with the times, but the principle—the spirit that underlies it—is the same that has slain the chosen of the Lord ever since the days of Abel.

As men seek to come into harmony with God, they will find that the offense of the cross has not ceased. Principalities and powers and wicked spirits in high places are arrayed against all who yield obedience to the law of heaven. Therefore, so far from causing grief, persecution should bring joy to the disciples of Christ, for it is an evidence that they are following in the steps of their Master.

While the Lord has not promised His people exemption from trials, He has promised that which is far better. He has said, "As thy days, so shall thy strength be." "My grace is sufficient for thee: for My strength is made perfect in weakness." Deuteronomy 33:25; 2 Corinthians 12:9. If you are called to go through the fiery furnace for His sake, Jesus will be by your side even as He was with the faithful three in Babylon. Those who love their Redeemer will rejoice at every opportunity of sharing with Him humiliation and reproach. The love they bear their Lord makes suffering for His sake sweet.

In all ages Satan has persecuted the people of God. He has tortured them and put them to death, but in dying they became conquerors. They revealed in their steadfast faith a mightier One than Satan. Satan could torture and kill the body, but he could not touch the life that was hid with Christ in God. He could incarcerate in prison walls, but he could not bind the spirit. They could look beyond the gloom to the glory, saying, "I reckon that the sufferings of this present time are not worthy to be compared with the glory which shall be revealed in us." "Our light affliction, which is but for a moment, worketh for us a far more exceeding and eternal weight of glory." Romans 8:18; 2 Corinthians 4:17.

Through trials and persecution, the glory—character—of God is revealed in His chosen ones. The church of God, hated and persecuted by the world, are educated and disciplined in the school of Christ. They walk in narrow paths on earth; they are purified in the furnace of affliction. They follow Christ through sore conflicts; they endure self-denial and experience bitter disappointments; but their painful experience teaches them the guilt and woe of sin, and they look upon it with abhorrence. Being partakers of Christ's sufferings, they are destined to be partakers of His glory. In holy vision the prophet saw the triumph of the people of God. He says, "I saw as it were a sea of glass mingled with fire: and them that had gotten the victory, ... stand on the sea of glass, having the harps of God. And they sing the song of Moses the servant of God, and the song of the Lamb, saying, Great and marvelous are Thy works, Lord God Almighty; just and true are Thy ways, Thou King of saints." "These are they which came out of great tribulation, and have washed their robes, and made them white in the blood of the Lamb. Therefore are they before the throne of God, and serve Him day and night in His temple: and He that sitteth on the throne shall dwell among them." Revelation 15:2, 3; 7:14, 15.

"Blessed are ye, when men shall revile you."—Matthew 5:11.

Ever since his fall, Satan has worked by means of deception. As he has misrepresented God, so, through his agents, he misrepresents the children of God. The Saviour says, "The reproaches of them that reproached Thee are fallen upon Me." Psalm 69:9. In like manner they fall upon His disciples.

There was never one who walked among men more cruelly slandered than the Son of man. He was derided and mocked because of His unswerving obedience to the principles of God's holy law. They hated Him without a cause. Yet He stood calmly before His enemies, declaring that reproach is a part of the Christian's legacy, counseling His followers how to meet the arrows of malice, bidding them not to faint under persecution.

While slander may blacken the reputation, it cannot stain the character. That is in God's keeping. So long as we do not consent to sin, there is no power, whether human or satanic, that can bring a stain upon the soul. A man whose heart is stayed upon God is just the same in the hour of his most afflicting trials and most discouraging surroundings as when he was in prosperity, when the light and favor of God seemed to be upon him. His words, his motives, his actions, may be misrepresented and falsified, but he does not mind it, because he has greater interests at stake. Like Moses, he endures as "seeing Him who is invisible" (Hebrews 11:27); looking "not at the things which are seen, but at the things which are not seen" (2 Corinthians 4:18).

Christ is acquainted with all that is misunderstood and misrepresented by men. His children can afford to wait in calm patience and trust, no matter how much maligned and despised; for nothing is secret that shall not be made manifest, and those who honor God shall be honored by Him in the presence of men and angels.

"When men shall revile you, and persecute you," said Jesus, "rejoice, and be exceeding glad." And He pointed His hearers to the prophets who had spoken in the name of the Lord, as "an example of suffering affliction, and of patience." James 5:10. Abel, the very first Christian of Adam's children, died a martyr. Enoch walked with God, and the world knew him not. Noah was mocked as a fanatic and an alarmist. "Others had trial of cruel mockings and scourgings, yea, moreover of bonds and imprisonment." "Others were tortured, not accepting deliverance; that they might obtain a better resurrection." Hebrews 11:36, 35.

In every age God's chosen messengers have been reviled and persecuted, yet through their affliction the knowledge of God has been spread abroad. Every disciple of Christ is to step into the ranks and carry forward the same work, knowing that its foes can do nothing against the truth, but for the truth. God means that truth shall be brought to the front and become the subject of examination and discussion, even through the contempt placed upon it. The minds of the people must be agitated; every controversy, every reproach, every effort to restrict liberty of conscience, is God's means of awakening minds that otherwise might slumber.

How often this result has been seen in the history of God's messengers! When the noble and eloquent Stephen was stoned to death at the instigation of the Sanhedrin council, there was no loss to the cause of the gospel. The light of heaven that glorified his face, the divine compassion breathed in his dying prayer, were as a sharp arrow of conviction to the bigoted Sanhedrist who stood by, and Saul, the persecuting Pharisee, became a chosen vessel to bear the name of Christ before Gentiles and kings and the children of Israel. And long afterward Paul the aged wrote from his prison house at Rome: "Some indeed preach Christ even of envy and strife: ... not sincerely, supposing to add affliction to my bonds.... Notwithstanding, every way, whether in pretense, or in truth, Christ is preached." Philippians 1:15-18. Through Paul's imprisonment the gospel was spread abroad, and souls were won for Christ in the very palace of the Caesars. By the efforts of Satan to destroy it, the "incorruptible" seed of the word of God, "which liveth and abideth forever" (1 Peter 1:23), is sown in the hearts of men; through the reproach and persecution of His children the name of Christ is magnified and souls are saved.

Great is the reward in heaven of those who are witnesses for Christ through persecution and reproach. While the people are looking for earthly good, Jesus points them to a heavenly reward. But He does not place it all in the future life; it begins here. The Lord appeared of old time to Abraham and said, "*I am thy shield, and thy exceeding great reward.*" Genesis 15:1. This is the reward of all who follow Christ. Jehovah Immanuel—He "in whom are hid all the treasures of wisdom and knowledge," in whom dwells "all the fullness of the Godhead bodily" (Colossians 2:3, 9)—to be brought into sympathy with Him, to know Him, to possess Him, as the heart opens more and more to receive His attributes; to know His love and power, to possess the unsearchable riches of Christ, to comprehend more and more "what is the breadth, and length, and depth, and height; and to know the love of Christ, which passeth knowledge, that ye might be filled with all the fullness of God" (Ephesians 3:18, 19)—"this is the heritage of the servants of the Lord, and their righteousness is of Me, saith the Lord." Isaiah 54:17.

It was this joy that filled the hearts of Paul and Silas when they prayed and sang praises to God at midnight in the Philippian dungeon. Christ was beside them there, and the light of His presence irradiated the gloom with the glory of the courts above. From Rome, Paul wrote, unmindful of his fetters as he saw the spread of the gospel, "I therein do rejoice, yea, and will rejoice." Philippians 1:18. And the very words of Christ upon the mount are re-echoed in Paul's message to the Philippian church, in the midst of their persecutions, "Rejoice in the Lord alway: and again I say, Rejoice." Philippians 4:4.

"Ye are the salt of the earth."—Matthew 5:13.

Salt is valued for its preservative properties; and when God calls His children salt, He would teach them that His purpose in making them the subjects of His grace is that they may become agents in saving others. The object of God in choosing a people before all the world was not only that He might adopt them as His sons and daughters, but that through them the world might receive the grace that bringeth salvation. Titus 2:11. When the Lord chose Abraham, it was not simply to be the special friend of God, but to be a medium of the peculiar privileges the Lord desired to bestow upon the nations. Jesus, in that last prayer with His disciples before His crucifixion, said, "For their sakes I sanctify Myself, that they also might be sanctified through the truth." John 17:19. In like manner Christians who are purified through the truth will possess saving qualities that preserve the world from utter moral corruption.

Salt must be mingled with the substance to which it is added; it must penetrate and infuse in order to preserve. So it is through personal contact and association that men are reached by the saving power of the gospel. They are not saved in masses, but as individuals. Personal influence is a power. We must come close to those whom we desire to benefit.

The savor of the salt represents the vital power of the Christian—the love of Jesus in the heart, the righteousness of Christ pervading the life. The love of Christ is diffusive and aggressive. If it is dwelling in us, it will flow out to others. We shall come close to them till their hearts are warmed by our unselfish interest and love. The sincere believers diffuse vital energy, which is penetrating and imparts new moral power to the souls for whom they labor. It is not the power of the man himself, but the power of the Holy Spirit that does the transforming work.

Jesus added the solemn warning: "If the salt have lost his savor, wherewith shall it be salted? It is thenceforth good for nothing, but to be cast out, and to be trodden under foot of men."

As they listened to the words of Christ, the people could see the white salt glistening in the pathways where it had been cast out because it had lost its savor and was therefore useless. It well represented the condition of the Pharisees and the effect of their religion upon society. It represents the life of every soul from whom the power of the grace of God has departed and who has become cold and Christless. Whatever may be his profession, such a one is looked upon by men and angels as insipid and disagreeable. It is to such that Christ says: "I would thou wert cold or hot. So then because thou art lukewarm, and neither cold nor hot, I will spue thee out of My mouth." Revelation 3:15, 16.

Without a living faith in Christ as a personal Saviour it is impossible to make our influence felt in a skeptical world. We cannot give to others that which we do not ourselves possess. It is in proportion to our own devotion and consecration to Christ that we exert an influence for the blessing and uplifting of mankind. If there is no actual service, no genuine love, no reality of experience, there is no power to help, no connection with heaven, no savor of Christ in the life. Unless the Holy Spirit can use us as agents through whom to communicate to the world the truth as it is in Jesus, we are as salt that has lost its savor and is entirely worthless. By our lack of the grace of Christ we testify to the world that the truth which we claim to believe has no sanctifying power; and thus, so far as our influence goes, we make of no effect the word of God. "If I speak with the tongues of men and of angels, but have not love, I am become sounding brass, or a clanging cymbal. And if I have the gift of prophecy, and know all mysteries and all knowledge; and if I have all faith, so as to remove mountains, but have not love, I am nothing. And if I bestow all my goods to feed the poor, and if I give my body to be burned, but have not love, it profiteth me nothing." 1 Corinthians 13:1-3 , A.R.V.

When love fills the heart, it will flow out to others, not because of favors received from them, but because love is the principle of action. Love modifies the character, governs the impulses, subdues enmity, and ennobles the affections. This love is as broad as the universe, and is in harmony with that of the angel workers. Cherished in the heart, it sweetens the entire life and sheds its blessing upon all around. It is this, and this only, that can make us the salt of the earth.

"Ye are the light of the world."—Matthew 5:14.

As Jesus taught the people, He made His lessons interesting and held the attention of His hearers by frequent illustrations from the scenes of nature about them. The people had come together while it was yet morning. The glorious sun, climbing higher and higher in the blue sky, was chasing away the shadows that lurked in the valleys and among the narrow defiles of the mountains. The glory of the eastern heavens had not yet faded out. The sunlight flooded the land with its splendor; the placid surface of the lake reflected the golden light and mirrored the rosy clouds of morning. Every bud and flower and leafy spray glistened with dewdrops. Nature smiled under the benediction of a new day, and the birds sang sweetly among the trees. The Saviour looked upon the company before Him, and then to the rising sun, and said to His disciples, "Ye are the light of the world." As the sun goes forth on its errand of love, dispelling the shades of night and awakening the world to life, so the followers of Christ are to go forth on their mission, diffusing the light of heaven upon those who are in the darkness of error and sin.

In the brilliant light of the morning, the towns and villages upon the surrounding hills stood forth clearly, making an attractive feature of the scene. Pointing to them, Jesus said, "A city set on a hill cannot be hid." And He added, "Neither do men light a lamp, and put it under the bushel, but on the stand; and it shineth unto all that are in the house." R.V. Most of those who listened to the words of Jesus were peasants and fishermen whose lowly dwellings contained but one room, in which the single lamp on its stand shone to all in the house. Even so, said Jesus, "Let your light so shine before men, that they may see your good works, and glorify your Father which is in heaven."

No other light ever has shone or ever will shine upon fallen man save that which emanates from Christ. Jesus, the Saviour, is the only light that can illuminate the darkness of a world lying in sin. Of Christ it is written, "In Him was life; and the life was the light of men." John 1:4. It was by receiving of His life that His disciples could become light bearers. The life of Christ in the soul, His love revealed in the character, would make them the light of the world.

Humanity has in itself no light. Apart from Christ we are like an unkindled taper, like the moon when her face is turned away from the sun; we have not a single ray of brightness to shed into the darkness of the world. But when we turn toward the Sun of Righteousness, when we come in touch with Christ, the whole soul is aglow with the brightness of the divine presence.

Christ's followers are to be more than a light in the midst of men. They are *the* light of the world. Jesus says to all who have named His name, You have given yourselves to Me, and I have given you to the world as My representatives. As the Father had sent Him into the world, so, He declares, "have I also sent them into the world." John 17:18. As Christ is the channel for the revelation of the Father, so we are to be the channel for the revelation of Christ. While our Saviour is the great source of illumination, forget not, O Christian, that He is revealed through humanity. God's blessings are bestowed through human instrumentality. Christ Himself came to the world as the Son of man. Humanity, united to the divine nature, must touch humanity. The church of Christ, every individual disciple of the Master, is heaven's appointed channel for the revelation of God to men. Angels of glory wait to communicate through you heaven's light and power to souls that are ready to perish. Shall the human agent fail of accomplishing his appointed work? Oh, then to that degree is the world robbed of the promised influence of the Holy Spirit!

But Jesus did not bid the disciples, "Strive to *make* your light shine;" He said, "*Let* it shine." If Christ is dwelling in the heart, it is impossible to conceal the light of His presence. If those who profess to be followers of Christ are not the light of the world, it is because the vital power has left them; if they have no light to give, it is because they have no connection with the Source of light.

In all ages the "Spirit of Christ which was in them" (1 Peter 1:11) has made God's true children the light of the people of their generation. Joseph was a light bearer in Egypt. In his purity and benevolence and filial love he represented Christ in the midst of a nation of idolaters. While the Israelites were on their way from Egypt to the Promised Land, the true-hearted among them were a light to the surrounding nations. Through them God was revealed to the world. From Daniel and his companions in Babylon, and from Mordecai in Persia, bright beams of light shone out amid the darkness of the kingly courts. In like manner the disciples of Christ are set as light bearers on the way to heaven; through them the Father's mercy and goodness are made manifest to a world enshrouded in the darkness of misapprehension of God. By seeing their good works, others are led to glorify the Father who is above; for it is made manifest that there is a God on the throne of the universe whose character is worthy of praise and imitation. The divine love glowing in the heart, the Christlike harmony manifested in the life, are as a glimpse of heaven granted to men of the world, that they may appreciate its excellence.

It is thus that men are led to believe "the love that God hath to us." 1 John 4:16. Thus hearts once sinful and corrupt are purified and transformed, to be presented "faultless before the presence of His glory with exceeding joy." Jude 24.

The Saviour's words, "Ye are the light of the world," point to the fact that He has committed to His followers a world-wide mission. In the days of Christ, selfishness and pride and prejudice had built strong and high the wall of partition between the appointed guardians of the sacred oracles and every other nation on the globe. But the Saviour had come to change all this. The words which the people were hearing from His lips were unlike anything to which they had ever listened from priest or rabbi. Christ tears away the wall of partition, the self-love, the dividing prejudice of nationality, and teaches a love for all the human family. He lifts men from the narrow circle that their selfishness prescribes; He abolishes all territorial lines and artificial distinctions of society. He makes no difference between neighbors and strangers, friends and enemies. He teaches us to look upon every needy soul as our neighbor and the world as our field.

As the rays of the sun penetrate to the remotest corners of the globe, so God designs that the light of the gospel shall extend to every soul upon the earth. If the church of Christ were fulfilling the purpose of our Lord, light would be shed upon all that sit in darkness and in the region and shadow of death. Instead of congregating together and shunning responsibility and cross bearing, the members of the church would scatter into all lands, letting the light of Christ shine out from them, working as He did for the salvation of souls, and this "gospel of the kingdom" would speedily be carried to all the world.

It is thus that God's purpose in calling His people, from Abraham on the plains of Mesopotamia to us in this age, is to reach its fulfillment. He says, "I will bless thee, ... and thou shalt be a blessing." Genesis 12:2. The words of Christ through the gospel prophet, which are but re-echoed in the Sermon on the Mount, are for us in this last generation: "Arise, shine; for thy light is come, and the glory of the Lord is risen upon thee." Isaiah 60:1. If upon your spirit the glory of the Lord is risen, if you have beheld His beauty who is "the chiefest among ten thousand" and the One "altogether lovely," if your soul has become radiant in the presence of His glory, to you is this word from the Master sent. Have you stood with Christ on the mount of transfiguration? Down in the plain there are souls enslaved by Satan; they are waiting for the word of faith and prayer to set them free.

We are not only to contemplate the glory of Christ, but also to speak of His excellences. Isaiah not only beheld the glory of Christ, but he also spoke of Him. While David mused, the fire burned; then spoke he with his tongue. While he mused upon the wondrous love of God he could not but speak of that which he saw and felt. Who can by faith behold the wonderful plan of redemption, the glory of the only-begotten Son of God, and not speak of it? Who can contemplate the unfathomable love that was manifested upon the cross of Calvary in the death of Christ, that we might not perish, but have everlasting life—who can behold this and have no words with which to extol the Saviour's glory?

"In His temple doth everyone speak of His glory." Psalm 29:9. The sweet singer of Israel praised Him upon the harp, saying, "I will speak of the glorious honor of Thy majesty, and of Thy wondrous works. And men shall speak of the might of Thy terrible acts: and I will declare Thy greatness." Psalm 145:5, 6.

The cross of Calvary is to be lifted high above the people, absorbing their minds and concentrating their thoughts. Then all the spiritual faculties will be charged with divine power direct from God. Then there will be a concentration of the energies in genuine work for the Master. The workers will send forth to the world beams of light, as living agencies to enlighten the earth.

Christ accepts, oh, so gladly, every human agency that is surrendered to Him. He brings the human into union with the divine, that He may communicate to the world the mysteries of incarnate love. Talk it, pray it, sing it; proclaim abroad the message of His glory, and keep pressing onward to the regions beyond.

Trials patiently borne, blessings gratefully received, temptations manfully resisted, meekness, kindness, mercy, and love habitually revealed, are the lights that shine forth in the character in contrast with the darkness of the selfish heart, into which the light of life has never shone.

Chapter 3—The Spirituality of the Law

"I am not come to destroy, but to fulfill."—Matthew 5:17.

It was Christ who, amid thunder and flame, had proclaimed the law upon Mount Sinai. The glory of God, like devouring fire, rested upon its summit, and the mountain quaked at the presence of the Lord. The hosts of Israel, lying prostrate upon the earth, had listened in awe to the sacred precepts of the law. What a contrast to the scene upon the mount of the Beatitudes! Under the summer sky, with no sound to break the stillness but the song of birds, Jesus unfolded the principles of His kingdom. Yet He who spoke to the people that day in accents of love, was opening to them the principles of the law proclaimed upon Sinai.

When the law was given, Israel, degraded by the long bondage in Egypt, had need to be impressed with the power and majesty of God; yet He revealed Himself to them no less as a God of love.

> "The Lord came from Sinai,
>   And rose from Seir unto them;
> He shined forth from Mount Paran,
>   And He came from the ten thousands of holy ones:
> At His right hand was a fiery law unto them.
>   Yea, He loveth the tribes;
> All their holy ones are in Thy hand:
>   And they sat down at Thy feet;
> Everyone received of Thy words."
>
>   Deuteronomy 33:2, 3 ,
>   R.V., margin.

It was to Moses that God revealed His glory in those wonderful words that have been the treasured heritage of the ages: "The Lord, The Lord God, merciful and gracious, long-suffering, and abundant in goodness and truth, keeping mercy for thousands, forgiving iniquity and transgression and sin." Exodus 34:6, 7.

The law given upon Sinai was the enunciation of the principle of love, a revelation to earth of the law of heaven. It was ordained in the hand of a Mediator—spoken by Him through whose power the hearts of men could be brought into harmony with its principles. God had revealed the purpose of the law when He declared to Israel, "Ye shall be holy men unto Me." Exodus 22:31.

But Israel had not perceived the spiritual nature of the law, and too often their professed obedience was but an observance of forms and ceremonies, rather than a surrender of the heart to the sovereignty of love. As Jesus in His character and work represented to men the holy, benevolent, and paternal attributes of God, and presented the worthlessness of mere ceremonial obedience, the Jewish leaders did not receive or understand His words. They thought that He dwelt too lightly upon the requirements of the law; and when He set before them the very truths that were the soul of their divinely appointed service, they, looking only at the external, accused Him of seeking to overthrow it.

The words of Christ, though calmly spoken, were uttered with an earnestness and power that stirred the hearts of the people. They listened for a repetition of the lifeless traditions and exactions of the rabbis, but in vain. They "were astonished at His teaching: for He taught them as one having authority, and not as their scribes." Matthew 7:29, R.V. The Pharisees noted the vast difference between their manner of instruction and that of Christ. They saw that the majesty and purity and beauty of the truth, with its deep and gentle influence, was taking firm hold upon many minds. The Saviour's divine love and tenderness drew the hearts of men to Him. The rabbis saw that by His teaching the whole tenor of the instruction they had given to the people was set at nought. He was tearing down the partition wall that had been so flattering to their pride and exclusiveness; and they feared that, if permitted, He would draw the people entirely away from them. Therefore they followed Him with determined hostility, hoping to find some occasion for bringing Him into disfavor with the multitudes and thus enabling the Sanhedrin to secure His condemnation and death.

[47]

On the mount, Jesus was closely watched by spies; and as He unfolded the principles of righteousness, the Pharisees caused it to be whispered about that His teaching was in opposition to the precepts that God had given from Sinai. The Saviour said nothing to unsettle faith in the religion and institutions that had been given through Moses; for every ray of divine light that Israel's great leader communicated to his people was received from Christ. While many are saying in their hearts that He has come to do away with the law, Jesus in unmistakable language reveals His attitude toward the divine statutes. "Think not," He said, "that I am come to destroy the law, or the prophets."

It is the Creator of men, the Giver of the law, who declares that it is not His purpose to set aside its precepts. Everything in nature, from the mote in the sunbeam to the worlds on high, is under law. And upon obedience to these laws the order and harmony of the natural world depend. So there are great principles of righteousness to control the life of all intelligent beings, and upon conformity to these principles the well-being of the universe depends. Before this earth was called into being, God's law existed. Angels are governed by its principles, and in order for earth to be in harmony with heaven, man also must obey the divine statutes. To man in Eden Christ made known the precepts of the law "when the morning stars sang together, and all the sons of God shouted for joy." Job 38:7. The mission of Christ on earth was not to destroy the law, but by His grace to bring man back to obedience to its precepts.

The beloved disciple, who listened to the words of Jesus on the mount, writing long afterward under the inspiration of the Holy Spirit, speaks of the law as of perpetual obligation. He says that "sin is the transgression of the law" and that "whosoever committeth sin transgresseth also the law." 1 John 3:4. He makes it plain that the law to which he refers is "an old commandment which ye had from the beginning." 1 John 2:7. He is speaking of the law that existed at the creation and was reiterated upon Mount Sinai.

Speaking of the law, Jesus said, "I am not come to destroy, but to fulfill." He here used the word "fulfill" in the same sense as when He declared to John the Baptist His purpose to "fulfill all righteousness" (Matthew 3:15); that is, to fill up the measure of the law's requirement, to give an example of perfect conformity to the will of God.

His mission was to "magnify the law, and make it honorable." Isaiah 42:21. He was to show the spiritual nature of the law, to present its far-reaching principles, and to make plain its eternal obligation.

The divine beauty of the character of Christ, of whom the noblest and most gentle among men are but a faint reflection; of whom Solomon by the Spirit of inspiration wrote, He is "the chiefest among ten thousand, ... yea, He is altogether lovely" (Song of Solomon 5:10-16); of whom David, seeing Him in prophetic vision, said, "Thou art fairer than the children of men" (Psalm 45:2); Jesus, the express image of the Father's person, the effulgence of His glory; the self-denying Redeemer, throughout His pilgrimage of love on earth, was a living representation of the character of the law of God. In His life it is made manifest that heaven-born love, Christlike principles, underlie the laws of eternal rectitude.

"Till heaven and earth pass," said Jesus, "one jot or one tittle shall in nowise pass from the law, till all be fulfilled." By His own obedience to the law, Christ testified to its immutable character and proved that through His grace it could be perfectly obeyed by every son and daughter of Adam. On the mount He declared that not the smallest iota should pass from the law till all things should be accomplished—all things that concern the human race, all that relates to the plan of redemption. He does not teach that the law is ever to be abrogated, but He fixes the eye upon the utmost verge of man's horizon and assures us that until this point is reached the law will retain its authority so that none may suppose it was His mission to abolish the precepts of the law. So long as heaven and earth continue, the holy principles of God's law will remain. His righteousness, "like the great mountains" (Psalm 36:6), will continue, a source of blessing, sending forth streams to refresh the earth.

[50]

Because the law of the Lord is perfect, and therefore changeless, it is impossible for sinful men, in themselves, to meet the standard of its requirement. This was why Jesus came as our Redeemer. It was His mission, by making men partakers of the divine nature, to bring them into harmony with the principles of the law of heaven. When we forsake our sins and receive Christ as our Saviour, the law is exalted. The apostle Paul asks, "Do we then make void the law through faith? God forbid: yea, we establish the law." Romans 3:31.

The new-covenant promise is, "I will put My laws into their hearts, and in their minds will I write them." Hebrews 10:16. While the system of types which pointed to Christ as the Lamb of God that should take away the sin of the world was to pass away at His death, the principles of righteousness embodied in the Decalogue are as immutable as the eternal throne. Not one command has been annulled, not a jot or tittle has been changed. Those principles that were made known to man in Paradise as the great law of life will exist unchanged in Paradise restored. When Eden shall bloom on earth again, God's law of love will be obeyed by all beneath the sun.

"Forever, O Lord, Thy word is settled in heaven." "All His commandments are sure. They stand fast for ever and ever, and are done in truth and uprightness." "Concerning Thy testimonies, I have known of old that Thou hast founded them forever." Psalm 119:89; 111:7, 8; Psalm 119:152.

"Whosoever ... shall break one of these least commandments, and shall teach men so, he shall be called the least in the kingdom of heaven."—Matthew 5:19.

That is, he shall have no place therein. For he who willfully breaks one commandment, does not, in spirit and truth, keep any of them. "Whosoever shall keep the whole law, and yet offend in one point, he is guilty of all." James 2:10.

It is not the greatness of the act of disobedience that constitutes sin, but the fact of variance from God's expressed will in the least particular; for this shows that there is yet communion between the soul and sin. The heart is divided in its service. There is a virtual denial of God, a rebellion against the laws of His government.

Were men free to depart from the Lord's requirements and to set up a standard of duty for themselves, there would be a variety of standards to suit different minds and the government would be taken out of the Lord's hands. The will of man would be made supreme, and the high and holy will of God—His purpose of love toward His creatures—would be dishonored, disrespected.

Whenever men choose their own way, they place themselves in controversy with God. They will have no place in the kingdom of heaven, for they are at war with the very principles of heaven. In disregarding the will of God, they are placing themselves on the side of Satan, the enemy of God and man. Not by one word, not by many words, but by every word that God has spoken, shall man live. We cannot disregard one word, however trifling it may seem to us, and be safe. There is not a commandment of the law that is not for the good and happiness of man, both in this life and in the life to come. In obedience to God's law, man is surrounded as with a hedge and kept from the evil. He who breaks down this divinely erected barrier at one point has destroyed its power to protect him; for he has opened a way by which the enemy can enter to waste and ruin.

By venturing to disregard the will of God upon one point, our first parents opened the floodgates of woe upon the world. And every individual who follows their example will reap a similar result. The love of God underlies every precept of His law, and he who departs from the commandment is working his own unhappiness and ruin.

"Except your righteousness shall exceed the righteousness of the scribes and Pharisees, ye shall in no case enter into the kingdom of heaven."—Matthew 5:20. [53]

The scribes and Pharisees had accused not only Christ but His disciples as sinners because of their disregard of the rabbinical rites and observances. Often the disciples had been perplexed and troubled by censure and accusation from those whom they had been accustomed to revere as religious teachers. Jesus unveiled the deception. He declared that the righteousness upon which the Pharisees set so great value was worthless. The Jewish nation had claimed to be the special, loyal people who were favored of God; but Christ represented their religion as devoid of saving faith. All their pretensions of piety, their human inventions and ceremonies, and even their boasted performance of the outward requirements of the law, could not avail to make them holy. They were not pure in heart or noble and Christlike in character.

A legal religion is insufficient to bring the soul into harmony with God. The hard, rigid orthodoxy of the Pharisees, destitute of contrition, tenderness, or love, was only a stumbling block to sinners. They were like the salt that had lost its savor; for their influence had no power to preserve the world from corruption. The only true faith is that which "worketh by love" (Galatians 5:6) to purify the soul. It is as leaven that transforms the character.

[54] All this the Jews should have learned from the teachings of the prophets. Centuries before, the cry of the soul for justification with God had found voice and answer in the words of the prophet Micah: "Wherewith shall I come before the Lord, and bow myself before the high God? shall I come before Him with burnt offerings, with calves of a year old? Will the Lord be pleased with thousands of rams, or with ten thousands of rivers of oil? ... He hath showed thee, O man, what is good; and what doth the Lord require of thee, but to do justly, and to love mercy, and to walk humbly with thy God?" Micah 6:6-8.

The prophet Hosea had pointed out what constitutes the very essence of Pharisaism, in the words, "Israel is an empty vine, he bringeth forth fruit unto himself." Hosea 10:1. In their professed service to God, the Jews were really working for self. Their righteousness was the fruit of their own efforts to keep the law according to their own ideas and for their own selfish benefit. Hence it could be no better than they were. In their endeavor to make themselves holy, they were trying to bring a clean thing out of an unclean. The law of God is as holy as He is holy, as perfect as He is perfect. It presents to men the righteousness of God. It is impossible for man, of himself, to keep this law; for the nature of man is depraved, deformed, and wholly unlike the character of God. The works of the selfish heart are "as an unclean thing;" and "all our righteousnesses are as filthy rags." Isaiah 64:6.

While the law is holy, the Jews could not attain righteousness by their own efforts to keep the law. The disciples of Christ must obtain [55] righteousness of a different character from that of the Pharisees, if they would enter the kingdom of heaven. God offered them, in His Son, the perfect righteousness of the law. If they would open their hearts fully to receive Christ, then the very life of God, His love, would dwell in them, transforming them into His own likeness; and thus through God's free gift they would possess the righteousness which the law requires. But the Pharisees rejected Christ; "being ignorant of God's righteousness, and going about to establish their own righteousness" (Romans 10:3), they would not submit themselves unto the righteousness of God.

Jesus proceeded to show His hearers what it means to keep the commandments of God—that it is a reproduction in themselves of the character of Christ. For in Him, God was daily made manifest before them.

"Everyone who is angry with his brother shall be in danger of the judgment."—Matthew 5:22, R. V.

Through Moses the Lord had said, "Thou shalt not hate thy brother in thine heart.... Thou shalt not avenge, nor bear any grudge against the children of thy people, but thou shalt love thy neighbor as thyself." Leviticus 19:17, 18. The truths which Christ presented were the same that had been taught by the prophets, but they had become obscured through hardness of heart and love of sin.

The Saviour's words revealed to His hearers the fact that, while they were condemning others as transgressors, they were themselves equally guilty; for they were cherishing malice and hatred.

Across the sea from the place where they were assembled was the country of Bashan, a lonely region, whose wild gorges and wooded hills had long been a favorite lurking ground for criminals of all descriptions. Reports of robbery and murder committed there were fresh in the minds of the people, and many were zealous in denouncing these evildoers. At the same time they were themselves passionate and contentious; they cherished the most bitter hatred of their Roman oppressors and felt themselves at liberty to hate and despise all other peoples, and even their own countrymen who did not in all things conform to their ideas. In all this they were violating the law which declares, "Thou shalt not kill."

The spirit of hatred and revenge originated with Satan, and it led him to put to death the Son of God. Whoever cherishes malice or unkindness is cherishing the same spirit, and its fruit will be unto death. In the revengeful thought the evil deed lies enfolded, as the plant in the seed. "Whosoever hateth his brother is a murderer: and ye know that no murderer hath eternal life abiding in him." 1 John 3:15.

"Whosoever shall say to his brother, Raca [vain fellow], shall be in danger of the council." In the gift of His Son for our redemption, God has shown how high a value He places upon every human soul, and He gives to no man liberty to speak contemptuously of another. We shall see faults and weaknesses in those about us, but God claims every soul as His property—His by creation, and doubly His as purchased by the precious blood of Christ. All were created in His image, and even the most degraded are to be treated with respect and tenderness. God will hold us accountable for even a word spoken in contempt of one soul for whom Christ laid down His life.

"Who maketh thee to differ from another? and what hast thou that thou didst not receive? now if thou didst receive it, why dost thou glory, as if thou hadst not received it?" "Who art thou that judgest another man's servant? to his own master he standeth or falleth." 1 Corinthians 4:7; Romans 14:4.

"Whosoever shall say, Thou fool, shall be in danger of the hell of fire." R.V. In the Old Testament the word "fool" is used to designate an apostate, or one who has abandoned himself to wickedness. Jesus says that whoever shall condemn his brother as an apostate or a despiser of God shows that he himself is worthy of the same condemnation.

Christ Himself, when contending with Satan about the body of Moses, "durst not bring against him a railing accusation." Jude 9. Had He done this, He would have placed Himself on Satan's ground, for accusation is the weapon of the evil one. He is called in Scripture, "the accuser of our brethren." Revelation 12:10. Jesus would employ none of Satan's weapons. He met him with the words, "The Lord rebuke thee." Jude 9.

His example is for us. When we are brought in conflict with the enemies of Christ, we should say nothing in a spirit of retaliation or that would bear even the appearance of a railing accusation. He who stands as a mouthpiece for God should not utter words which even the Majesty of heaven would not use when contending with Satan. We are to leave with God the work of judging and condemning.

"Be reconciled to thy brother."—Matthew 5:24.

The love of God is something more than a mere negation; it is a positive and active principle, a living spring, ever flowing to bless others. If the love of Christ dwells in us, we shall not only cherish no hatred toward our fellows, but we shall seek in every way to manifest love toward them.

Jesus said, "If thou bring thy gift to the altar, and there rememberest that thy brother hath aught against thee; leave there thy gift before the altar, and go thy way; first be reconciled to thy brother, and then come and offer thy gift." The sacrificial offerings expressed faith that through Christ the offerer had become a partaker of the mercy and love of God. But for one to express faith in God's pardoning love, while he himself indulged an unloving spirit, would be a mere farce.

When one who professes to serve God wrongs or injures a brother, he misrepresents the character of God to that brother, and the wrong must be confessed, he must acknowledge it to be sin, in order to be in harmony with God. Our brother may have done us a greater wrong than we have done him, but this does not lessen our responsibility. If when we come before God we remember that another has aught against us, we are to leave our gift of prayer, of thanksgiving, of freewill offering, and go to the brother with whom we are at variance, and in humility confess our own sin and ask to be forgiven.

[59]

If we have in any manner defrauded or injured our brother, we should make restitution. If we have unwittingly borne false witness, if we have misstated his words, if we have injured his influence in any way, we should go to the ones with whom we have conversed about him, and take back all our injurious misstatements.

If matters of difficulty between brethren were not laid open before others, but frankly spoken of between themselves in the spirit of Christian love, how much evil might be prevented! How many roots of bitterness whereby many are defiled would be destroyed, and how closely and tenderly might the followers of Christ be united in His love!

"Whosoever looketh on a woman to lust after her hath committed adultery with her already in his heart."—Matthew 5:28.

The Jews prided themselves on their morality and looked with horror upon the sensual practices of the heathen. The presence of the

Roman officers whom the imperial rule had brought into Palestine was a continual offense to the people, for with these foreigners had come in a flood of heathen customs, lust, and dissipation. In Capernaum, Roman officials with their gay paramours haunted the parades and promenades, and often the sound of revelry broke upon the stillness of the lake as their pleasure boats glided over the quiet waters. The people expected to hear from Jesus a stern denunciation of this class, but what was their astonishment as they listened to words that laid bare the evil of their own hearts!

When the thought of evil is loved and cherished, however secretly, said Jesus, it shows that sin still reigns in the heart. The soul is still in the gall of bitterness and in the bond of iniquity. He who finds pleasure in dwelling upon scenes of impurity, who indulges the evil thought, the lustful look, may behold in the open sin, with its burden of shame and heart-breaking grief, the true nature of the evil which he has hidden in the chambers of the soul. The season of temptation, under which, it may be, one falls into grievous sin, does not create the evil that is revealed, but only develops or makes manifest that which was hidden and latent in the heart. As a man "thinketh in his heart, so is he;" for out of the heart "are the issues of life." Proverbs 23:7; 4:23.

"If thy right hand causeth thee to stumble, cut it off, and cast it from thee."—Matthew 5:30, R. V.

To prevent disease from spreading to the body and destroying life, a man would submit to part even with his right hand. Much more should he be willing to surrender that which imperils the life of the soul.

Through the gospel, souls that are degraded and enslaved by Satan are to be redeemed to share the glorious liberty of the sons of God. God's purpose is not merely to deliver from the suffering that is the inevitable result of sin, but to save from sin itself. The soul, corrupted and deformed, is to be purified, transformed, that it may be clothed in "the beauty of the Lord our God," "conformed to the image of His Son." "Eye hath not seen, nor ear heard, neither have entered into the heart of man, the things which God hath prepared for them that love Him." Psalm 90:17; Romans 8:29; 1 Corinthians

2:9. Eternity alone can reveal the glorious destiny to which man, restored to God's image, may attain.

In order for us to reach this high ideal, that which causes the soul to stumble must be sacrificed. It is through the will that sin retains its hold upon us. The surrender of the will is represented as plucking out the eye or cutting off the hand. Often it seems to us that to surrender the will to God is to consent to go through life maimed or crippled. But it is better, says Christ, for self to be maimed, wounded, crippled, if thus you may enter into life. That which you look upon as disaster is the door to highest benefit.

God is the fountain of life, and we can have life only as we are in communion with Him. Separated from God, existence may be ours for a little time, but we do not possess life. "She that liveth in pleasure is dead while she liveth." 1 Timothy 5:6. Only through the surrender of our will to God is it possible for Him to impart life to us. Only by receiving His life through self-surrender is it possible, said Jesus, for these hidden sins, which I have pointed out, to be overcome. It is possible that you may bury them in your hearts and conceal them from human eyes, but how will you stand in God's presence?

[62]

If you cling to self, refusing to yield your will to God, you are choosing death. To sin, wherever found, God is a consuming fire. If you choose sin, and refuse to separate from it, the presence of God, which consumes sin, must consume you.

It will require a sacrifice to give yourself to God; but it is a sacrifice of the lower for the higher, the earthly for the spiritual, the perishable for the eternal. God does not design that our will should be destroyed, for it is only through its exercise that we can accomplish what He would have us do. Our will is to be yielded to Him, that we may receive it again, purified and refined, and so linked in sympathy with the Divine that He can pour through us the tides of His love and power. However bitter and painful this surrender may appear to the willful, wayward heart, yet "it is profitable for thee."

Not until he fell crippled and helpless upon the breast of the covenant angel did Jacob know the victory of conquering faith and receive the title of a prince with God. It was when he "halted upon his thigh" (Genesis 32:31) that the armed bands of Esau were stilled before him, and the Pharaoh, proud heir of a kingly line, stooped to crave his blessing. So the Captain of our salvation was made "perfect through sufferings" (Hebrews 2:10), and the children of faith "out of weakness were made strong," and "turned to flight the armies of the aliens" (Hebrews 11:34). So do "the lame take the prey" (Isaiah 33:23), and the weak become "as David," and "the house of David ... as the angel of the Lord" (Zechariah 12:8).

"Is it lawful for a man to put away his wife?"—Matthew 19:3.

Among the Jews a man was permitted to put away his wife for the most trivial offenses, and the woman was then at liberty to marry again. This practice led to great wretchedness and sin. In the Sermon on the Mount Jesus declared plainly that there could be no dissolution of the marriage tie, except for unfaithfulness to the marriage vow. "Everyone," He said, "that putteth away his wife, saving for the cause of fornication, maketh her an adulteress: and whosoever shall marry her when she is put away committeth adultery." R.V.

When the Pharisees afterward questioned Him concerning the lawfulness of divorce, Jesus pointed His hearers back to the marriage institution as ordained at creation. "Because of the hardness of your hearts," He said, Moses "suffered you to put away your wives: but from the beginning it was not so." Matthew 19:8. He referred them to the blessed days of Eden, when God pronounced all things "very good." Then marriage and the Sabbath had their origin, twin institutions for the glory of God in the benefit of humanity. Then, as the Creator joined the hands of the holy pair in wedlock, saying, A man shall "leave his father and his mother, and shall cleave unto his wife: and they shall be one" (Genesis 2:24), He enunciated the law of marriage for all the children of Adam to the close of time. That which the Eternal Father Himself had pronounced good was the law of highest blessing and development for man.

Like every other one of God's good gifts entrusted to the keeping of humanity, marriage has been perverted by sin; but it is the purpose of the gospel to restore its purity and beauty. In both the Old and the New Testament the marriage relation is employed to represent the tender and sacred union that exists between Christ and His people, the redeemed ones whom He has purchased at the cost of Calvary.

"Fear not," He says; "thy Maker is thine husband; the Lord of hosts is His name; and thy Redeemer, the Holy One of Israel." "Turn, O backsliding children, saith the Lord; for I am married unto you." Isaiah 54:4, 5; Jeremiah 3:14. In the "Song of Songs" we hear the bride's voice saying, "My Beloved is mine, and I am His." And He who is to her "the chiefest among ten thousand," speaks to His chosen one, "Thou art all fair, My love; there is no spot in thee." Song of Solomon 2:16; 5:10; 4:7.

In later times Paul the apostle, writing to the Ephesian Christians, declares that the Lord has constituted the husband the head of the wife, to be her protector, the house-band, binding the members of the family together, even as Christ is the head of the church and the Saviour of the mystical body. Therefore he says, "As the church is subject unto Christ, so let the wives be to their own husbands in everything. Husbands, love your wives, even as Christ also loved the church, and gave Himself for it; that He might sanctify and cleanse it with the washing of water by the word, that He might present it to Himself a glorious church, not having spot, or wrinkle, or any such thing; but that it should be holy and without blemish. So ought men to love their wives." Ephesians 5:24-28.

[65]

The grace of Christ, and this alone, can make this institution what God designed it should be—an agent for the blessing and uplifting of humanity. And thus the families of earth, in their unity and peace and love, may represent the family of heaven.

Now, as in Christ's day, the condition of society presents a sad comment upon heaven's ideal of this sacred relation. Yet even for those who have found bitterness and disappointment where they had hoped for companionship and joy, the gospel of Christ offers a solace. The patience and gentleness which His Spirit can impart will sweeten the bitter lot. The heart in which Christ dwells will be so filled, so satisfied, with His love that it will not be consumed with longing to attract sympathy and attention to itself. And through the surrender of the soul to God, His wisdom can accomplish what human wisdom fails to do. Through the revelation of His grace, hearts that were once indifferent or estranged may be united in bonds that are firmer and more enduring than those of earth—the golden bonds of a love that will bear the test of trial.

"Swear not at all."—Matthew 5:34.

The reason for this command is given: We are not to swear "by the heaven, for it is the throne of God; nor by the earth, for it is the footstool of His feet; nor by Jerusalem, for it is the city of the great King. Neither shalt thou swear by thy head, for thou canst not make one hair white or black." R.V.

All things come of God. We have nothing that we have not received; and, more than this, we have nothing that has not been purchased for us by the blood of Christ. Everything we possess comes to us stamped with the cross, bought with the blood that is precious above all estimate, because it is the life of God. Hence there is nothing that we have a right to pledge, as if it were our own, for the fulfillment of our word.

The Jews understood the third commandment as prohibiting the profane use of the name of God; but they thought themselves at liberty to employ other oaths. Oath taking was common among them. Through Moses they had been forbidden to swear falsely, but they had many devices for freeing themselves from the obligation imposed by an oath. They did not fear to indulge in what was really profanity, nor did they shrink from perjury so long as it was veiled by some technical evasion of the law.

Jesus condemned their practices, declaring that their custom in oath taking was a transgression of the commandment of God. Our Saviour did not, however, forbid the use of the judicial oath, in which God is solemnly called to witness that what is said is truth and nothing but the truth. Jesus Himself, at His trial before the Sanhedrin, did not refuse to testify under oath. The high priest said unto Him, "I adjure Thee by the living God, that Thou tell us whether Thou be the Christ, the Son of God." Jesus answered, "Thou hast said." Matthew 26:63, 64. Had Christ in the Sermon on the Mount condemned the judicial oath, He would at His trial have reproved the high priest and thus, for the benefit of His followers, have enforced His own teaching.

There are very many who do not fear to deceive their fellow men, but they have been taught, and have been impressed by the Spirit of God, that it is a fearful thing to lie to their Maker. When put under oath they are made to feel that they are not testifying merely before men, but before God; that if they bear false witness, it is to Him who reads the heart and who knows the exact truth. The knowledge of the fearful judgments that have followed this sin has a restraining influence upon them.

But if there is anyone who can consistently testify under oath, it is the Christian. He lives constantly as in the presence of God, knowing that every thought is open to the eyes of Him with whom we have to do; and when required to do so in a lawful manner, it is right for him to appeal to God as a witness that what he says is the truth, and nothing but the truth.

Jesus proceeded to lay down a principle that would make oath taking needless. He teaches that the exact truth should be the law of speech. "Let your speech be, Yea, yea; Nay, nay: and whatsoever is more than these is of the evil one." R.V.

These words condemn all those meaningless phrases and expletives that border on profanity. They condemn the deceptive compliments, the evasion of truth, the flattering phrases, the exaggerations, the misrepresentations in trade, that are current in society and in the business world. They teach that no one who tries to appear what he is not, or whose words do not convey the real sentiment of his heart, can be called truthful. [68]

If these words of Christ were heeded, they would check the utterance of evil surmising and unkind criticism; for in commenting upon the actions and motives of another, who can be certain of speaking the exact truth? How often pride, passion, personal resentment, color the impression given! A glance, a word, even an intonation of the voice, may be vital with falsehood. Even facts may be so stated as to convey a false impression. And "whatsoever is more than" truth, "is of the evil one."

Everything that Christians do should be as transparent as the sunlight. Truth is of God; deception, in every one of its myriad forms, is of Satan; and whoever in any way departs from the straight line of truth is betraying himself into the power of the wicked one. Yet it is not a light or an easy thing to speak the exact truth. We cannot speak the truth unless we know the truth; and how often preconceived opinions, mental bias, imperfect knowledge, errors of judgment, prevent a right understanding of matters with which we have to do! We cannot speak the truth unless our minds are continually guided by Him who is truth.

[69] Through the apostle Paul, Christ bids us, "Let your speech be alway with grace." "Let no corrupt communication proceed out of your mouth, but that which is good to the use of edifying, that it may minister grace unto the hearers." Colossians 4:6; Ephesians 4:29. In the light of these scriptures the words of Christ upon the mount are seen to condemn jesting, trifling, and unchaste conversation. They require that our words should be not only truthful, but pure.

Those who have learned of Christ will "have no fellowship with the unfruitful works of darkness." Ephesians 5:11. In speech, as in life, they will be simple, straightforward, and true; for they are preparing for the fellowship of those holy ones in whose mouth "was found no guile." Revelation 14:5.

"Resist not him that is evil: but whosoever smiteth thee on thy right cheek, turn to him the other also."—Matthew 5:39, R. V.

Occasions of irritation to the Jews were constantly arising from their contact with the Roman soldiery. Detachments of troops were stationed at different points throughout Judea and Galilee, and their presence reminded the people of their own degradation as a nation. With bitterness of soul they heard the loud blast of the trumpet and saw the troops forming around the standard of Rome and bowing in homage to this symbol of her power. Collisions between the people and the soldiers were frequent, and these inflamed the popular hatred. Often as some Roman official with his guard of soldiers hastened [70] from point to point, he would seize upon the Jewish peasants who were laboring in the field and compel them to carry burdens up the mountainside or render any other service that might be needed. This was in accordance with the Roman law and custom, and resistance to such demands only called forth taunts and cruelty. Every day deepened in the hearts of the people the longing to cast off the Roman yoke. Especially among the bold, rough-handed Galileans the spirit of insurrection was rife. Capernaum, being a border town, was the seat of a Roman garrison, and even while Jesus was teaching, the sight of a company of soldiers recalled to His hearers the bitter thought of Israel's humiliation. The people looked eagerly to Christ, hoping that He was the One who was to humble the pride of Rome.

With sadness Jesus looks into the upturned faces before Him. He notes the spirit of revenge that has stamped its evil imprint upon them, and knows how bitterly the people long for power to crush their oppressors. Mournfully He bids them, "Resist not him that is evil: but whosoever smiteth thee on thy right cheek, turn to him the other also."

These words were but a reiteration of the teaching of the Old Testament. It is true that the rule, "Eye for eye, tooth for tooth" (Leviticus 24:20), was a provision in the laws given through Moses; but it was a civil statute. None were justified in avenging themselves, for they had the words of the Lord: "Say not thou, I will recompense evil." "Say not, I will do so to him as he hath done to me." "Rejoice not when thine enemy falleth." "If he that hateth thee be hungry, give him bread to eat; and if he be thirsty, give him water to drink." Proverbs 20:22; 24:29, 17; Proverbs 25:21, 22, R.V., margin.

The whole earthly life of Jesus was a manifestation of this principle. It was to bring the bread of life to His enemies that our Saviour left His home in heaven. Though calumny and persecution were heaped upon Him from the cradle to the grave, they called forth from Him only the expression of forgiving love. Through the prophet Isaiah He says, "I gave My back to the smiters, and My cheeks to them that plucked off the hair: I hid not My face from shame and spitting." "He was oppressed, and He was afflicted, yet He opened not His mouth: He is brought as a lamb to the slaughter, and as a sheep before her shearers is dumb, so He openeth not His mouth." Isaiah 50:6; 53:7. And from the cross of Calvary there come down through the ages His prayer for His murderers and the message of hope to the dying thief.

The Father's presence encircled Christ, and nothing befell Him but that which infinite love permitted for the blessing of the world. Here was His source of comfort, and it is for us. He who is imbued with the Spirit of Christ abides in Christ. The blow that is aimed at him falls upon the Saviour, who surrounds him with His presence. Whatever comes to him comes from Christ. He has no need to resist evil, for Christ is his defense. Nothing can touch him except by our

[71]

Lord's permission, and "all things" that are permitted "work together for good to them that love God." Romans 8:28.

[72] "If any man would go to law with thee, and take away thy coat [tunic], let him have thy cloak [mantle] also. And whosoever shall impress thee to go one mile, go with him twain." R.V., margin.

Jesus bade His disciples, instead of resisting the demands of those in authority, to do even more than was required of them. And, so far as possible, they should discharge every obligation, even if it were beyond what the law of the land required. The law, as given through Moses, enjoined a very tender regard for the poor. When a poor man gave his garment as a pledge, or as security for a debt, the creditor was not permitted to enter the dwelling to obtain it; he must wait in the street for the pledge to be brought to him. And whatever the circumstances the pledge must be returned to its owner at nightfall. Deuteronomy 24:10-13. In the days of Christ these merciful provisions were little regarded; but Jesus taught His disciples to submit to the decision of the court, even though this should demand more than the law of Moses authorized. Though it should demand a part of their raiment, they were to yield. More than this, they were to give to the creditor his due, if necessary surrendering even more than the court gave him authority to seize. "If any man would go to law with thee," He said, "and take away thy coat, let him have thy cloak also." R.V. And if the couriers require you to go a mile with them, go two miles.

Jesus added, "Give to him that asketh thee, and from him that would borrow of thee turn not thou away." The same lesson had been taught through Moses: "Thou shalt not harden thine heart, nor shut [73] thine hand from thy poor brother: but thou shalt open thine hand wide unto him, and shalt surely lend him sufficient for his need, in that which he wanteth." Deuteronomy 15:7, 8. This scripture makes plain the meaning of the Saviour's words. Christ does not teach us to give indiscriminately to all who ask for charity; but He says, "Thou shalt surely lend him sufficient for his need;" and this is to be a gift, rather than a loan; for we are to "lend, hoping for nothing again.".

> "Who gives himself with his alms feeds three,
> Himself, his hungering neighbor, and Me."

"Love your enemies."—Matthew 5:44.

The Saviour's lesson, "Resist not him that is evil," was a hard saying for the revengeful Jews, and they murmured against it among themselves. But Jesus now made a still stronger declaration:

"Ye have heard that it hath been said, Thou shalt love thy neighbor, and hate thine enemy. But I say unto you, Love your enemies, bless them that curse you, do good to them that hate you, and pray for them which despitefully use you and persecute you; that ye may be the children of your Father which is in heaven."

Such was the spirit of the law which the rabbis had misinterpreted as a cold and rigid code of exactions. They regarded themselves as better than other men, and as entitled to the special favor of God by virtue of their birth as Israelites; but Jesus pointed to the spirit of forgiving love as that which would give evidence that they were actuated by any higher motives than even the publicans and sinners, whom they despised.

[74]

He pointed His hearers to the Ruler of the universe, under the new name, "Our Father." He would have them understand how tenderly the heart of God yearned over them. He teaches that God cares for every lost soul; that "like as a father pitieth his children, so the Lord pitieth them that fear Him." Psalm 103:13. Such a conception of God was never given to the world by any religion but that of the Bible. Heathenism teaches men to look upon the Supreme Being as an object of fear rather than of love—a malign deity to be appeased by sacrifices, rather than a Father pouring upon His children the gift of His love. Even the people of Israel had become so blinded to the precious teaching of the prophets concerning God that this revelation of His paternal love was as an original subject, a new gift to the world.

The Jews held that God loved those who served Him,—according to their view, those who fulfilled the requirements of the rabbis,—and that all the rest of the world lay under His frown and curse. Not so, said Jesus; the whole world, the evil and the good, lies in the sunshine of His love. This truth you should have learned from nature itself; for God "maketh His sun to rise on the evil and on the good, and sendeth rain on the just and on the unjust."

It is not because of inherent power that year by year the earth produces her bounties and continues her motion round the sun. The hand of God guides the planets and keeps them in position in their orderly march through the heavens. It is through His power that summer and winter, seedtime and harvest, day and night follow each other in their regular succession. It is by His word that vegetation flourishes, that the leaves appear and the flowers bloom. Every good thing we have, each ray of sunshine and shower of rain, every morsel of food, every moment of life, is a gift of love.

While we were yet unloving and unlovely in character, "hateful, and hating one another," our heavenly Father had mercy on us. "After that the kindness and love of God our Saviour toward man appeared, not by works of righteousness which we have done, but according to His mercy He saved us." Titus 3:3-5. His love received, will make us, in like manner, kind and tender, not merely toward those who please us, but to the most faulty and erring and sinful.

The children of God are those who are partakers of His nature. It is not earthly rank, nor birth, nor nationality, nor religious privilege, which proves that we are members of the family of God; it is love, a love that embraces all humanity. Even sinners whose hearts are not utterly closed to God's Spirit, will respond to kindness; while they may give hate for hate, they will also give love for love. But it is only the Spirit of God that gives love for hatred. To be kind to the unthankful and to the evil, to do good hoping for nothing again, is the insignia of the royalty of heaven, the sure token by which the children of the Highest reveal their high estate.

"Be ye therefore perfect, even as your Father which is in heaven is perfect."—Matthew 5:48.

The word "therefore" implies a conclusion, an inference from what has gone before. Jesus has been describing to His hearers the unfailing mercy and love of God, and He bids them therefore to be perfect. Because your heavenly Father "is kind unto the unthankful and to the evil" (Luke 6:35), because He has stooped to lift you up, therefore, said Jesus, you may become like Him in character, and stand without fault in the presence of men and angels.

The conditions of eternal life, under grace, are just what they were in Eden—perfect righteousness, harmony with God, perfect conformity to the principles of His law. The standard of character presented in the Old Testament is the same that is presented in the New Testament. This standard is not one to which we cannot attain. In every command or injunction that God gives there is a promise, the most positive, underlying the command. God has made provision that we may become like unto Him, and He will accomplish this for all who do not interpose a perverse will and thus frustrate His grace.

With untold love our God has loved us, and our love awakens toward Him as we comprehend something of the length and breadth and depth and height of this love that passeth knowledge. By the revelation of the attractive loveliness of Christ, by the knowledge of His love expressed to us while we were yet sinners, the stubborn heart is melted and subdued, and the sinner is transformed and becomes a child of heaven. God does not employ compulsory measures; love is the agent which He uses to expel sin from the heart. By it He changes pride into humility, and enmity and unbelief into love and faith.

[77]

The Jews had been wearily toiling to reach perfection by their own efforts, and they had failed. Christ had already told them that their righteousness could never enter the kingdom of heaven. Now He points out to them the character of the righteousness that all who enter heaven will possess. Throughout the Sermon on the Mount He describes its fruits, and now in one sentence He points out its source and its nature: Be perfect as God is perfect. The law is but a transcript of the character of God. Behold in your heavenly Father a perfect manifestation of the principles which are the foundation of His government.

God is love. Like rays of light from the sun, love and light and joy flow out from Him to all His creatures. It is His nature to give. His very life is the outflow of unselfish love.

> "His glory is His children's good;
> His joy, His tender Fatherhood."

He tells us to be perfect as He is, in the same manner. We are to be centers of light and blessing to our little circle, even as He is to the universe. We have nothing of ourselves, but the light of His love shines upon us, and we are to reflect its brightness. "In His borrowed goodness good," we may be perfect in our sphere, even as God is perfect in His.

[78]   Jesus said, Be perfect as *your Father* is perfect. If you are the children of God you are partakers of His nature, and you cannot but be like Him. Every child lives by the life of his father. If you are God's children, begotten by His Spirit, you live by the life of God. In Christ dwells "all the fullness of the Godhead bodily" (Colossians 2:9); and the life of Jesus is made manifest "in our mortal flesh" (2 Corinthians 4:11). That life in you will produce the same character and manifest the same works as it did in Him. Thus you will be in harmony with every precept of His law; for "the law of the Lord is perfect, restoring the soul." Psalm 19:7 , margin. Through love "the righteousness of the law" will be "fulfilled in us, who walk not after the flesh, but after the Spirit." Romans 8:4.

Chapter 4—The True Motive in Service

"Take heed that ye do not your righteousness before men, to be seen of them."—Matthew 6:1, margin.

The words of Christ on the mount were an expression of that which had been the unspoken teaching of His life, but which the people had failed to comprehend. They could not understand how, having such great power, He neglected to use it in securing what they regarded as the chief good. Their spirit and motives and methods were the opposite of His. While they claimed to be very jealous for the honor of the law, self-glory was the real object which they sought; and Christ would make it manifest to them that the lover of self is a transgressor of the law.

But the principles cherished by the Pharisees are such as are characteristic of humanity in all ages. The spirit of Pharisaism is the spirit of human nature; and as the Saviour showed the contrast between His own spirit and methods and those of the rabbis, His teaching is equally applicable to the people of all time.

In the days of Christ the Pharisees were continually trying to earn the favor of Heaven in order to secure the worldly honor and prosperity which they regarded as the reward of virtue. At the same time they paraded their acts of charity before the people in order to attract their attention and gain a reputation for sanctity.

Jesus rebuked their ostentation, declaring that God does not recognize such service and that the flattery and admiration of the people, which they so eagerly sought, was the only reward they would ever receive.

"When thou doest alms," He said, "let not thy left hand know what thy right hand doeth: that thine alms may be in secret: and thy Father which seeth in secret Himself shall reward thee openly."

In these words Jesus did not teach that acts of kindness should always be kept secret. Paul the apostle, writing by the Holy Spirit, did not conceal the generous self-sacrifice of the Macedonian Christians, but told of the grace that Christ had wrought in them, and thus others were imbued with the same spirit. He also wrote to the church at Corinth and said, "Your zeal hath stirred up very many." 2 Corinthians 9:2 , R.V.

Christ's own words make His meaning plain, that in acts of charity the aim should not be to secure praise and honor from men. Real godliness never prompts an effort at display. Those who desire words of praise and flattery, and feed upon them as a sweet morsel, are Christians in name only.

By their good works, Christ's followers are to bring glory, not to themselves, but to Him through whose grace and power they have wrought. It is through the Holy Spirit that every good work is accomplished, and the Spirit is given to glorify, not the receiver, but the Giver. When the light of Christ is shining in the soul, the lips will be filled with praise and thanksgiving to God. Your prayers, your performance of duty, your benevolence, your self-denial, will not be the theme of your thought or conversation. Jesus will be magnified, self will be hidden, and Christ will appear as all in all.

We are to give in sincerity, not to make a show of our good deeds, but from pity and love to the suffering ones. Sincerity of purpose, real kindness of heart, is the motive that Heaven values. The soul that is sincere in its love, wholehearted in its devotion, God regards as more precious than the golden wedge of Ophir.

We are not to think of reward, but of service; yet kindness shown in this spirit will not fail of its recompense. "Thy Father which seeth in secret Himself shall reward thee openly." While it is true that God Himself is the great Reward, that embraces every other, the soul receives and enjoys Him only as it becomes assimilated to Him in character. Only like can appreciate like. It is as we give ourselves to God for the service of humanity that He gives Himself to us.

No one can give place in his own heart and life for the stream of God's blessing to flow to others, without receiving in himself a rich reward. The hillsides and plains that furnish a channel for the mountain streams to reach the sea suffer no loss thereby. That which they give is repaid a hundredfold. For the stream that goes singing on its way leaves behind its gift of verdure and fruitfulness. The grass on its banks is a fresher green, the trees have a richer verdure, the flowers are more abundant. When the earth lies bare and brown under the summer's parching heat, a line of verdure marks the river's course; and the plain that opened her bosom to bear the mountain's treasure to the sea is clothed with freshness and beauty, a witness to the recompense that God's grace imparts to all who give themselves as a channel for its outflow to the world.

This is the blessing of those who show mercy to the poor. The prophet Isaiah says, "Is it not to deal thy bread to the hungry, and that thou bring the poor that are cast out to thy house? when thou seest the naked, that thou cover him; and that thou hide not thyself from thine own flesh? Then shall thy light break forth as the morning, and thine health shall spring forth speedily.... And the Lord shall guide thee continually, and satisfy thy soul in drought: ... and thou shalt be like a watered garden, and like a spring of water, whose waters fail not." Isaiah 58:7-11.

The work of beneficence is twice blessed. While he that gives to the needy blesses others, he himself is blessed in a still greater degree. The grace of Christ in the soul is developing traits of character that are the opposite of selfishness,—traits that will refine, ennoble, and enrich the life. Acts of kindness performed in secret will bind hearts together, and will draw them closer to the heart of Him from whom every generous impulse springs. The little attentions, the small acts of love and self-sacrifice, that flow out from the life as quietly as the fragrance from a flower—these constitute no small share of the blessings and happiness of life. And it will be found at last that the denial of self for the good and happiness of others, however humble and uncommended here, is recognized in heaven as the token of our union with Him, the King of glory, who was rich, yet for our sake became poor.

The deeds of kindness may have been done in secret, but the result upon the character of the doer cannot be hidden. If we work with wholehearted interest as a follower of Christ, the heart will be in close sympathy with God, and the Spirit of God, moving upon our spirit, will call forth the sacred harmonies of the soul in answer to the divine touch.

He who gives increased talents to those who have made a wise improvement of the gifts entrusted to them is pleased to acknowledge the service of His believing people in the Beloved, through whose grace and strength they have wrought. Those who have sought for the development and perfection of Christian character by exercising their faculties in good works, will, in the world to come, reap that which they have sown. The work begun upon earth will reach its consummation in that higher and holier life to endure throughout eternity.

> **"When thou prayest, thou shalt not be as the hypocrites are."—Matthew 6:5.**

The Pharisees had stated hours for prayer; and when, as often came to pass, they were abroad at the appointed time, they would pause wherever they might be—perhaps in the street or the market place, amid the hurrying throngs of men—and there in a loud voice rehearse their formal prayers. Such worship, offered merely for self-glorification, called forth unsparing rebuke from Jesus. He did not, however, discountenance public prayer, for He Himself prayed with His disciples and in the presence of the multitude. But He teaches that private prayer is not to be made public. In secret devotion our prayers are to reach the ears of none but the prayer-hearing God. No curious ear is to receive the burden of such petitions.

"When thou prayest, enter into thy closet." Have a place for secret prayer. Jesus had select places for communion with God, and so should we. We need often to retire to some spot, however humble, where we can be alone with God.

"Pray to thy Father which is in secret." In the name of Jesus we may come into God's presence with the confidence of a child. No man is needed to act as a mediator. Through Jesus we may open our hearts to God as to one who knows and loves us.

In the secret place of prayer, where no eye but God's can see, no ear but His can hear, we may pour out our most hidden desires and longings to the Father of infinite pity, and in the hush and silence of the soul that voice which never fails to answer the cry of human need will speak to our hearts.

"The Lord is very pitiful, and of tender mercy." James 5:11. He waits with unwearied love to hear the confessions of the wayward and to accept their penitence. He watches for some return of gratitude from us, as the mother watches for the smile of recognition from her beloved child. He would have us understand how earnestly and tenderly His heart yearns over us. He invites us to take our trials to His sympathy, our sorrows to His love, our wounds to His healing, our weakness to His strength, our emptiness to His fullness. Never has one been disappointed who came unto Him. "They looked unto Him, and were lightened: and their faces were not ashamed." Psalm 34:5.

Those who seek God in secret telling the Lord their needs and pleading for help, will not plead in vain. "Thy Father which seeth in secret Himself shall reward thee openly." As we make Christ our daily companion we shall feel that the powers of an unseen world are all around us; and by looking unto Jesus we shall become assimilated to His image. By beholding we become changed. The character is softened, refined, and ennobled for the heavenly kingdom. The sure result of our intercourse and fellowship with our Lord will be to increase piety, purity, and fervor. There will be a growing intelligence in prayer. We are receiving a divine education, and this is illustrated in a life of diligence and zeal.

The soul that turns to God for its help, its support, its power, by daily, earnest prayer, will have noble aspirations, clear perceptions of truth and duty, lofty purposes of action, and a continual hungering and thirsting after righteousness. By maintaining a connection with God, we shall be enabled to diffuse to others, through our association with them, the light, the peace, the serenity, that rule in our hearts. The strength acquired in prayer to God, united with persevering effort in training the mind in thoughtfulness and care-taking, prepares one for daily duties and keeps the spirit in peace under all circumstances.

If we draw near to God, He will put a word in our mouth to speak for Him, even praise unto His name. He will teach us a strain from the song of the angels, even thanksgiving to our heavenly Father. In every act of life, the light and love of an indwelling Saviour will be revealed. Outward troubles cannot reach the life that is lived by faith in the Son of God.

> **"When ye pray, use not vain repetitions, as the heathen do."—Matthew 6:7.**

The heathen looked upon their prayers as having in themselves merit to atone for sin. Hence the longer the prayer the greater the merit. If they could become holy by their own efforts they would have something in themselves in which to rejoice, some ground for boasting. This idea of prayer is an outworking of the principle of self-expiation which lies at the foundation of all systems of false religion. The Pharisees had adopted this pagan idea of prayer, and it is by no means extinct in our day, even among those who profess to be Christians. The repetition of set, customary phrases, when the heart feels no need of God, is of the same character as the "vain repetitions" of the heathen.

Prayer is not an expiation for sin; it has no virtue or merit of itself. All the flowery words at our command are not equivalent to one holy desire. The most eloquent prayers are but idle words if they do not express the true sentiments of the heart. But the prayer that comes from an earnest heart, when the simple wants of the soul are expressed, as we would ask an earthly friend for a favor, expecting it to be granted—this is the prayer of faith. God does not desire our ceremonial compliments, but the unspoken cry of the heart broken and subdued with a sense of its sin and utter weakness finds its way to the Father of all mercy.

"When ye fast, be not, as the hypocrites."—Matthew 6:16.

The fasting which the word of God enjoins is something more than a form. It does not consist merely in refusing food, in wearing sackcloth, in sprinkling ashes upon the head. He who fasts in real sorrow for sin will never court display.

The object of the fast which God calls upon us to keep is not to afflict the body for the sin of the soul, but to aid us in perceiving the grievous character of sin, in humbling the heart before God and receiving His pardoning grace. His command to Israel was, "Rend your heart, and not your garments, and turn unto the Lord your God." Joel 2:13.

It will avail nothing for us to do penance or to flatter ourselves that by our own works we shall merit or purchase an inheritance among the saints. When the question was asked Christ, "What shall we do, that we might work the works of God?" He answered, "This is the work of God, that ye believe on Him whom He hath sent." John 6:28, 29. Repentance is turning from self to Christ; and when we receive Christ so that through faith He can live His life in us, good works will be manifest.

Jesus said, "When thou fastest, anoint thine head, and wash thy face; that thou appear not unto men to fast, but unto thy Father which is in secret." Matthew 6:17, 18. Whatever is done to the glory of God is to be done with cheerfulness, not with sadness and gloom. There is nothing gloomy in the religion of Jesus. If Christians give the impression by a mournful attitude that they have been disappointed in their Lord, they misrepresent His character and put arguments into the mouth of His enemies. Though in words they may claim God as their Father, yet in gloom and sorrow they present to the world the aspect of orphans.

Christ desires us to make His service appear attractive, as it really is. Let the self-denials and the secret heart trials be revealed to the compassionate Saviour. Let the burdens be left at the foot of the cross, and go on your way rejoicing in His love who first loved you. Men may never know of the work going on secretly between the soul and God, but the result of the Spirit's work upon the heart will be manifest to all, for He "which seeth in secret, shall reward thee openly."

"Lay not up for yourselves treasures upon earth."—Matthew 6:19.

Treasure laid up on earth will not endure; thieves break through and steal; moth and rust corrupt; fire and storm sweep away your possessions. And "where your treasure is, there will your heart be also." Treasure laid up on the earth will engross the mind to the exclusion of heavenly things.

The love of money was the ruling passion in the Jewish age. Worldliness usurped the place of God and religion in the soul. So it is now. Avaricious greed for wealth exerts such a fascinating, bewitching influence over the life that it results in perverting the nobility and corrupting the humanity of men until they are drowned in perdition. The service of Satan is full of care, perplexity, and wearing labor, and the treasure men toil to accumulate on earth is only for a season.

Jesus said, "Lay up for yourselves treasures in heaven, where neither moth nor rust doth corrupt, and where thieves do not break through nor steal: for where your treasure is, there will your heart be also."

The instruction is to "lay up for *yourselves* treasures in heaven." It is for your own interest to secure heavenly riches. These alone, of all that you possess, are really yours. The treasure laid up in heaven is imperishable. No fire or flood can destroy it, no thief despoil it, no moth or rust corrupt it; for it is in the keeping of God.

This treasure, which Christ esteems as precious above all estimate, is "the riches of the glory of His inheritance in the saints." Ephesians 1:18. The disciples of Christ are called His jewels, His precious and peculiar treasure. He says, "They shall be as the stones of a crown." "I will make a man more precious than fine gold; even a man than the golden wedge of Ophir." Zechariah 9:16; Isaiah 13:12. Christ looks upon His people in their purity and perfection as the reward of all His sufferings, His humiliation, and His love, and the supplement of His glory—Christ, the great Center, from whom radiates all glory.

[90] And we are permitted to unite with Him in the great work of redemption and to be sharers with Him in the riches which His death and suffering have won. The apostle Paul wrote to the Thessalonian Christians: "What is our hope, or joy, or crown of rejoicing? Are not even ye in the presence of our Lord Jesus Christ at His coming? for ye are our glory and joy." 1 Thessalonians 2:19, 20. This is the treasure for which Christ bids us labor. Character is the great harvest of life. And every word or deed that through the grace of Christ shall kindle in one soul an impulse that reaches heavenward, every effort that tends to the formation of a Christlike character, is laying up treasure in heaven.

Where the treasure is, there the heart will be. In every effort to benefit others, we benefit ourselves. He who gives money or time for spreading the gospel enlists his own interest and prayers for the work, and for the souls to be reached through it; his affections go out to others, and he is stimulated to greater devotion to God, that he may be enabled to do them the greatest good.

And at the final day, when the wealth of earth shall perish, he who has laid up treasure in heaven will behold that which his life has gained. If we have given heed to the words of Christ, then, as we gather around the great white throne, we shall see souls who have been saved through our agency, and shall know that one has saved others, and these still others—a large company brought into the haven of rest as the result of our labors, there to lay their crowns at Jesus' feet, and praise Him through the ceaseless ages of eternity. With what joy will the worker for Christ behold these redeemed ones, who share the glory of the Redeemer! How precious will heaven be to those who have been faithful in the work of saving souls!

"If ye then be risen with Christ, seek those things which are above, where Christ sitteth on the right hand of God." Colossians 3:1.

"If ... thine eye be single, thy whole body shall be full of light."—Matthew 6:22.

Singleness of purpose, wholehearted devotion to God, is the condition pointed out by the Saviour's words. Let the purpose be sincere and unwavering to discern the truth and to obey it at whatever cost, and you will receive divine enlightenment. Real piety begins when all compromise with sin is at an end. Then the language of the heart will be that of the apostle Paul: "This one thing I do, forgetting those things which are behind, and reaching forth unto those things which are before, I press toward the mark for the prize of the high calling of God in Christ Jesus." "I count all things but loss for the excellency of the knowledge of Christ Jesus my Lord: for whom I have suffered the loss of all things, and do count them but dung, that I may win Christ." Philippians 3:13, 14, 8.

But when the eye is blinded by the love of self, there is only darkness. "If thine eye be evil, thy whole body shall be full of darkness." It was this fearful darkness that wrapped the Jews in stubborn unbelief, making it impossible for them to appreciate the character and mission of Him who came to save them from their sins.

Yielding to temptation begins in permitting the mind to waver, to be inconstant in your trust in God. If we do not choose to give ourselves fully to God then we are in darkness. When we make any reserve we are leaving open a door through which Satan can enter to lead us astray by his temptations. He knows that if he can obscure our vision, so that the eye of faith cannot see God, there will be no barrier against sin.

The prevalence of a sinful desire shows the delusion of the soul. Every indulgence of that desire strengthens the soul's aversion to God. In following the path of Satan's choosing, we are encompassed by the shadows of evil, and every step leads into deeper darkness and increases the blindness of the heart.

The same law obtains in the spiritual as in the natural world. He who abides in darkness will at last lose the power of vision. He is shut in by a deeper than midnight blackness; and to him the brightest noontide can bring no light. He "walketh in darkness, and knoweth not whither he goeth, because that darkness hath blinded his eyes." 1 John 2:11. Through persistently cherishing evil, willfully disregarding the pleadings of divine love, the sinner loses the love for good, the desire for God, the very capacity to receive the light of heaven. The invitation of mercy is still full of love, the light is shining as brightly as when it first dawned upon his soul; but the voice falls on deaf ears, the light on blinded eyes.

[93] No soul is ever finally deserted of God, given up to his own ways, so long as there is any hope of his salvation. "Man turns from God, not God from him." Our heavenly Father follows us with appeals and warnings and assurances of compassion, until further opportunities and privileges would be wholly in vain. The responsibility rests with the sinner. By resisting the Spirit of God today, he prepares the way for a second resistance of light when it comes with mightier power. Thus he passes on from one stage of resistance to another, until at last the light will fail to impress, and he will cease to respond in any measure to the Spirit of God. Then even "the light that is in thee" has become darkness. The very truth we do know has become so perverted as to increase the blindness of the soul.

"No man can serve two masters."—Matthew 6:24.

Christ does not say that man will not or shall not serve two masters, but that he *cannot*. The interests of God and the interests of mammon have no union or sympathy. Just where the conscience of the Christian warns him to forbear, to deny himself, to stop, just there the worldling steps over the line, to indulge his selfish propensities. On one side of the line is the self-denying follower of Christ; on the other side is the self-indulgent world lover, pandering to fashion, engaging in frivolity, and pampering himself in forbidden pleasure. On that side of the line the Christian cannot go.

No one can occupy a neutral position; there is no middle class, who neither love God nor serve the enemy of righteousness. Christ is to live in His human agents and work through their faculties and act through their capabilities. Their will must be submitted to His will; they must act with His Spirit. Then it is no more they that live, but Christ that lives in them. He who does not give himself wholly to God is under the control of another power, listening to another voice, whose suggestions are of an entirely different character. Half-and-half service places the human agent on the side of the enemy as a successful ally of the hosts of darkness. When men who claim to be soldiers of Christ engage with the confederacy of Satan, and help along his side, they prove themselves enemies of Christ. They betray sacred trusts. They form a link between Satan and the true soldiers, so that through these agencies the enemy is constantly working to steal away the hearts of Christ's soldiers.

The strongest bulwark of vice in our world is not the iniquitous life of the abandoned sinner or the degraded outcast; it is that life which otherwise appears virtuous, honorable, and noble, but in which one sin is fostered, one vice indulged. To the soul that is struggling in secret against some giant temptation, trembling upon the very verge of the precipice, such an example is one of the most powerful enticements to sin. He who, endowed with high conceptions of life and truth and honor, does yet willfully transgress one precept of God's holy law, has perverted His noble gifts into a lure to sin. Genius, talent, sympathy, even generous and kindly deeds, may become decoys of Satan to entice other souls over the precipice of ruin for this life and the life to come.

"Love not the world, neither the things that are in the world. If any man love the world, the love of the Father is not in him. For all that is in the world, the lust of the flesh, and the lust of the eyes, and the pride of life, is not of the Father, but is of the world." 1 John 2:15, 16.

"Be not anxious."—Matthew 6:25, R. V.

He who has given you life knows your need of food to sustain it. He who created the body is not unmindful of your need of raiment. Will not He who has bestowed the greater gift bestow also what is needed to make it complete?

Jesus pointed His hearers to the birds as they warbled their carols of praise, unencumbered with thoughts of care, for "they sow not, neither do they reap;" and yet the great Father provides for their needs. And He asks, "Are not ye of much more value than they?" R.V.

> "No sparrow falls without His care,
>   No soul bows low but Jesus knows;
> For He is with us everywhere,
>   And marks each bitter tear that flows.
> And He will never, never, never
>   Forsake the soul that trusts Him ever."

The hillsides and the fields were bright with flowers, and, pointing to them in the dewy freshness of the morning, Jesus said, "Consider the lilies of the field, how they grow." The graceful forms and delicate hues of the plants and flowers may be copied by human skill, but what touch can impart life to even one flower or blade of grass? Every wayside blossom owes its being to the same power that set the starry worlds on high. Through all created things thrills one pulse of life from the great heart of God. The flowers of the field are clothed by His hand in richer robes than have ever graced the forms of earthly kings. And "if God so clothe the grass of the field, which today is, and tomorrow is cast into the oven, shall He not much more clothe you, O ye of little faith?"

It is He who made the flowers and who gave to the sparrow its song who says, "Consider the lilies," "Behold the birds." R.V. In the loveliness of the things of nature you may learn more of the wisdom of God than the schoolmen know. On the lily's petals, God has written a message for you, written in language that your heart can read only as it unlearns the lessons of distrust and selfishness and corroding care. Why has He given you the singing birds and the gentle blossoms, but from the overflowing love of a Father's heart, that would brighten and gladden your path of life? All that was needed for existence would have been yours without the flowers and birds, but God was not content to provide what would suffice for mere existence. He has filled earth and air and sky with glimpses of beauty to tell you of His loving thought for you. The beauty of all created things is but a gleam from the shining of His glory. If He has lavished such infinite skill upon the things of nature, for your happiness and joy, can you doubt that He will give you every needed blessing?

"Consider the lilies." Every flower that opens its petals to the sunshine obeys the same great laws that guide the stars, and how simple and beautiful and how sweet its life! Through the flowers, God would call our attention to the loveliness of Christlike character. He who has given such beauty to the blossoms desires far more that the soul should be clothed with the beauty of the character of Christ.

Consider, says Jesus, how the lilies grow; how, springing from the cold, dark earth, or from the mud of the river bed, the plants unfold in loveliness and fragrance. Who would dream of the possibilities of beauty in the rough brown bulb of the lily? But when the life of God, hidden therein, unfolds at His call in the rain and the sunshine, men marvel at the vision of grace and loveliness. Even so will the life of God unfold in every human soul that will yield itself to the ministry of His grace, which, free as the rain and the sunshine, comes with its benediction to all. It is the word of God that creates the flowers, and the same word will produce in you the graces of His Spirit.

God's law is the law of love. He has surrounded you with beauty to teach you that you are not placed on earth merely to delve for self, to dig and build, to toil and spin, but to make life bright and joyous and beautiful with the love of Christ—like the flowers, to gladden other lives by the ministry of love.

Fathers and mothers, let your children learn from the flowers. Take them with you into garden and field and under the leafy trees, and teach them to read in nature the message of God's love. Let the thoughts of Him be linked with bird and flower and tree. Lead the children to see in every pleasant and beautiful thing an expression of God's love for them. Recommend your religion to them by its pleasantness. Let the law of kindness be in your lips.

Teach the children that because of God's great love their natures may be changed and brought into harmony with His. Teach them that He would have their lives beautiful with the graces of the flowers. Teach them, as they gather the sweet blossoms, that He who made the flowers is more beautiful than they. Thus the tendrils of their hearts will be entwined about Him. He who is "altogether lovely" will become to them as a daily companion and familiar friend, and their lives will be transformed into the image of His purity.

"Seek ye first the kingdom of God."—Matthew 6:33.

The people who listened to the words of Christ were still anxiously watching for some announcement of the earthly kingdom. While Jesus was opening to them the treasures of heaven, the question uppermost in many minds was, How will a connection with Him advance our prospects in the world? Jesus shows that in making the things of the world their supreme anxiety they were like the heathen nations about them, living as if there were no God, whose tender care is over His creatures.

"All these things," said Jesus, "do the nations of the world seek after." "Your heavenly Father knoweth that ye have need of all these things. But seek ye first the kingdom of God, and His righteousness; and all these things shall be added unto you." Luke 12:30; Matthew 6:32, 33. I have come to open to you the kingdom of love and righteousness and peace. Open your hearts to receive this kingdom, and make its service your highest interest. Though it is a spiritual kingdom, fear not that your needs for this life will be uncared-for. If you give yourself to God's service, He who has all power in heaven and earth will provide for your needs.

Jesus does not release us from the necessity of effort, but He teaches that we are to make Him first and last and best in everything. We are to engage in no business, follow no pursuit, seek no pleasure, that would hinder the outworking of His righteousness in our character and life. Whatever we do is to be done heartily, as unto the Lord.

Jesus, while He dwelt on earth, dignified life in all its details by keeping before men the glory of God, and by subordinating everything to the will of His Father. If we follow His example, His assurance to us is that all things needful in this life "shall be added." Poverty or wealth, sickness or health, simplicity or wisdom—all are provided for in the promise of His grace.

God's everlasting arm encircles the soul that turns to Him for aid, however feeble that soul may be. The precious things of the hills shall perish, but the soul that lives for God shall abide with Him. "The world passeth away, and the lust thereof; but he that doeth the will of God abideth forever." 1 John 2:17. The city of God will open its golden gates to receive him who learned while on earth to lean on God for guidance and wisdom, for comfort and hope, amid loss and affliction. The songs of the angels will welcome him there, and for him the tree of life shall yield its fruit. "The mountains shall depart, and the hills be removed; but My kindness shall not depart from thee, neither shall the covenant of My peace be removed, saith the Lord that hath mercy on thee." Isaiah 54:10.

"Be not therefore anxious for the morrow.... Sufficient unto the day is the evil thereof."—Matthew 6:34, R. V.

If you have given yourself to God, to do His work, you have no need to be anxious for tomorrow. He whose servant you are, knows the end from the beginning. The events of tomorrow, which are hidden from your view, are open to the eyes of Him who is omnipotent.

When we take into our hands the management of things with which we have to do, and depend upon our own wisdom for success, we are taking a burden which God has not given us, and are trying to bear it without His aid. We are taking upon ourselves the responsibility that belongs to God, and thus are really putting ourselves in His place. We may well have anxiety and anticipate danger and loss, for it is certain to befall us. But when we really believe that God loves us and means to do us good we shall cease to worry about the future. We shall trust God as a child trusts a loving parent. Then our troubles and torments will disappear, for our will is swallowed up in the will of God.

Christ has given us no promise of help in bearing today the burdens of tomorrow. He has said, "My grace is sufficient for thee" (2 Corinthians 12:9); but, like the manna given in the wilderness,

His grace is bestowed daily, for the day's need. Like the hosts of Israel in their pilgrim life, we may find morning by morning the bread of heaven for the day's supply.

One day alone is ours, and during this day we are to live for God. For this one day we are to place in the hand of Christ, in solemn service, all our purposes and plans, casting all our care upon Him, for He careth for us. "I know the thoughts that I think toward you, saith the Lord, thoughts of peace, and not of evil, to give you an expected end." "In returning and rest shall ye be saved; in quietness and in confidence shall be your strength." Jeremiah 29:11; Isaiah 30:15.

If you will seek the Lord and be converted every day; if you will of your own spiritual choice be free and joyous in God; if with gladsome consent of heart to His gracious call you come wearing the yoke of Christ,—the yoke of obedience and service,—all your murmurings will be stilled, all your difficulties will be removed, all the perplexing problems that now confront you will be solved.

Chapter 5—The Lord's Prayer [102]

"After this manner therefore pray ye."—Matthew 6:9.

The Lord's Prayer was twice given by our Saviour, first to the multitude in the Sermon on the Mount, and again, some months later, to the disciples alone. The disciples had been for a short time absent from their Lord, when on their return they found Him absorbed in communion with God. Seeming unconscious of their presence, He continued praying aloud. The Saviour's face was irradiated with a celestial brightness. He seemed to be in the very presence of the Unseen, and there was a living power in His words as of one who spoke with God.

The hearts of the listening disciples were deeply moved. They had marked how often He spent long hours in solitude in communion with His Father. His days were passed in ministry to the crowds that pressed upon Him, and in unveiling the treacherous sophistry of the rabbis, and this incessant labor often left Him so utterly wearied that His mother and brothers, and even His disciples, had feared that His life would be sacrificed. But as He returned from the hours of prayer that closed the toilsome day, they marked the look of peace upon His face, the sense of refreshment that seemed to pervade His presence. It was from hours spent with God that He came forth, morning by morning, to bring the light of heaven to men. The disciples had come to connect His hours of prayer with the power [103] of His words and works. Now, as they listened to His supplication, their hearts were awed and humbled. As He ceased praying, it was with a conviction of their own deep need that they exclaimed, "Lord, teach us to pray." Luke 11:1.

Jesus gives them no new form of prayer. That which He has before taught them He repeats, as if He would say, You need to understand what I have already given. It has a depth of meaning you have not yet fathomed.

The Saviour does not, however, restrict us to the use of these exact words. As one with humanity, He presents His own ideal of prayer, words so simple that they may be adopted by the little child, yet so comprehensive that their significance can never be fully grasped by the greatest minds. We are taught to come to God with our tribute of thanksgiving, to make known our wants, to confess our sins, and to claim His mercy in accordance with His promise.

"When ye pray, say, Our Father."—Luke 11:2.

Jesus teaches us to call *His* Father our Father. He is not ashamed to call us brethren. Hebrews 2:11. So ready, so eager, is the Saviour's heart to welcome us as members of the family of God, that in the very first words we are to use in approaching God He places the assurance of our divine relationship, "Our Father."

Here is the announcement of that wonderful truth, so full of encouragement and comfort, that God loves us as He loves His Son. This is what Jesus said in His last prayer for His disciples, Thou "hast loved them, as Thou hast loved Me." John 17:23.

The world that Satan has claimed and has ruled over with cruel tyranny, the Son of God has, by one vast achievement, encircled in His love and connected again with the throne of Jehovah. Cherubim and seraphim, and the unnumbered hosts of all the unfallen worlds, sang anthems of praise to God and the Lamb when this triumph was assured. They rejoiced that the way of salvation had been opened to the fallen race and that the earth would be redeemed from the curse of sin. How much more should those rejoice who are the objects of such amazing love!

How can we ever be in doubt and uncertainty, and feel that we are orphans? It was in behalf of those who had transgressed the law that Jesus took upon Him human nature; He became like unto us, that we might have everlasting peace and assurance. We have an Advocate in the heavens, and whoever accepts Him as a personal Saviour is not left an orphan to bear the burden of his own sins.

"Beloved, now are we the sons of God." "And if children, then heirs; heirs of God, and joint heirs with Christ; if so be that we suffer with Him, that we may be also glorified together." "It doth not yet appear what we shall be: but we know that, when He shall appear, we shall be like Him; for we shall see Him as He is." 1 John 3:2; Romans 8:17.

The very first step in approaching God is to know and believe the love that He has to us (1 John 4:16); for it is through the drawing of His love that we are led to come to Him.

[105]

The perception of God's love works the renunciation of selfishness. In calling God our Father, we recognize all His children as our brethren. We are all a part of the great web of humanity, all members of one family. In our petitions we are to include our neighbors as well as ourselves. No one prays aright who seeks a blessing for himself alone.

The infinite God, said Jesus, makes it your privilege to approach Him by the name of Father. Understand all that this implies. No earthly parent ever pleaded so earnestly with an erring child as He who made you pleads with the transgressor. No human, loving interest ever followed the impenitent with such tender invitations. God dwells in every abode; He hears every word that is spoken, listens to every prayer that is offered, tastes the sorrows and disappointments of every soul, regards the treatment that is given to father, mother, sister, friend, and neighbor. He cares for our necessities, and His love and mercy and grace are continually flowing to satisfy our need.

But if you call God your Father you acknowledge yourselves His children, to be guided by His wisdom and to be obedient in all things, knowing that His love is changeless. You will accept His plan for your life. As children of God, you will hold His honor, His character, His family, His work, as the objects of your highest interest. It will be your joy to recognize and honor your relation to your Father and to every member of His family. You will rejoice to do any act, however humble, that will tend to His glory or to the well-being of your kindred.

[106]

"Which art in heaven." He to whom Christ bids us look as "our Father" "is in the heavens: He hath done whatsoever He hath pleased." In His care we may safely rest, saying, "What time I am afraid, I will trust in Thee." Psalm 115:3; 56:3.

"Hallowed be Thy name."—Matthew 6:9.

To hallow the name of the Lord requires that the words in which we speak of the Supreme Being be uttered with reverence. "Holy and reverend is His name." Psalm 111:9. We are never in any manner to treat lightly the titles or appellations of the Deity. In prayer we enter the audience chamber of the Most High; and we should come before Him with holy awe. The angels veil their faces in His presence. The cherubim and the bright and holy seraphim approach His throne with solemn reverence. How much more should we, finite, sinful beings, come in a reverent manner before the Lord, our Maker!

But to hallow the name of the Lord means much more than this. We may, like the Jews in Christ's day, manifest the greatest outward reverence for God, and yet profane His name continually. "The name of the Lord" is "merciful and gracious, long-suffering, and abundant in goodness and truth, ... forgiving iniquity and transgression and sin." Exodus 34:5-7. Of the church of Christ it is written, "This is the name wherewith she shall be called, The Lord our Righteousness." Jeremiah 33:16. This name is put upon every follower of Christ. It is the heritage of the child of God. The family are called after the Father. The prophet Jeremiah, in the time of Israel's sore distress and tribulation, prayed, "We are called by Thy name; leave us not." Jeremiah 14:9.

This name is hallowed by the angels of heaven, by the inhabitants of unfallen worlds. When you pray, "Hallowed be Thy name," you ask that it may be hallowed in this world, hallowed in you. God has acknowledged you before men and angels as His child; pray that you may do no dishonor to the "worthy name by which ye are called." James 2:7. God sends you into the world as His representative. In every act of life you are to make manifest the name of God. This petition calls upon you to possess His character. You cannot hallow His name, you cannot represent Him to the world, unless in life and character you represent the very life and character of God. This you can do only through the acceptance of the grace and righteousness of Christ.

Lord's Prayer

"Thy kingdom come."—Matthew 6:10.

God is our Father, who loves and cares for us as His children; He is also the great King of the universe. The interests of His kingdom are our interests, and we are to work for its upbuilding.

The disciples of Christ were looking for the immediate coming of the kingdom of His glory, but in giving them this prayer Jesus taught that the kingdom was not then to be established. They were to pray for its coming as an event yet future. But this petition was also an assurance to them. While they were not to behold the coming of the kingdom in their day, the fact that Jesus bade them pray for it is evidence that in God's own time it will surely come.

The kingdom of God's grace is now being established, as day by day hearts that have been full of sin and rebellion yield to the sovereignty of His love. But the full establishment of the kingdom of His glory will not take place until the second coming of Christ to this world. "The kingdom and dominion, and the greatness of the kingdom under the whole heaven," is to be given to "the people of the saints of the Most High." Daniel 7:27. They shall inherit the kingdom prepared for them "from the foundation of the world." Matthew 25:34. And Christ will take to Himself His great power and will reign.

The heavenly gates are again to be lifted up, and with ten thousand times ten thousand and thousands of thousands of holy ones, our Saviour will come forth as King of kings and Lord of lords. Jehovah Immanuel "shall be king over all the earth: in that day shall there be one Lord, and His name one." "The tabernacle of God" shall be with men, "and He will dwell with them, and they shall be His people, and God Himself shall be with them, and be their God." Zechariah 14:9; Revelation 21:3.

But before that coming, Jesus said, "This gospel of the kingdom shall be preached in all the world for a witness unto all nations." Matthew 24:14. His kingdom will not come until the good tidings of His grace have been carried to all the earth. Hence, as we give ourselves to God, and win other souls to Him, we hasten the coming of His kingdom. Only those who devote themselves to His service, saying, "Here am I; send me" (Isaiah 6:8), to open blind eyes, to turn men "from darkness to light and from the power of Satan unto God, that they may receive forgiveness of sins and inheritance among them which are sanctified" (Acts 26:18)—they alone pray in sincerity, "Thy kingdom come."

"Thy will be done in earth, as it is in heaven."—Matthew 6:10.

The will of God is expressed in the precepts of His holy law, and the principles of this law are the principles of heaven. The angels of heaven attain unto no higher knowledge than to know the will of God, and to do His will is the highest service that can engage their powers.

But in heaven, service is not rendered in the spirit of legality. When Satan rebelled against the law of Jehovah, the thought that there was a law came to the angels almost as an awakening to something unthought of. In their ministry the angels are not as servants, but as sons. There is perfect unity between them and their Creator. Obedience is to them no drudgery. Love for God makes their service a joy. So in every soul wherein Christ, the hope of glory, dwells, His words are re-echoed, "I delight to do Thy will, O My God: yea, Thy law is within My heart." Psalm 40:8.

[110] The petition, "Thy will be done in earth, as it is in heaven," is a prayer that the reign of evil on this earth may be ended, that sin may be forever destroyed, and the kingdom of righteousness be established. Then in earth as in heaven will be fulfilled "all the good pleasure of His goodness." 2 Thessalonians 1:11.

"Give us this day our daily bread."—Matthew 6:11.

The first half of the prayer Jesus has taught us is in regard to the name and kingdom and will of God—that His name may be honored, His kingdom established, His will performed. When you have thus made God's service your first interest, you may ask with confidence that your own needs may be supplied. If you have renounced self and given yourself to Christ you are a member of the family of God, and everything in the Father's house is for you. All the treasures of God are opened to you, both the world that now is and that which is to come. The ministry of angels, the gift of His Spirit, the labors of His servants—all are for you. The world, with everything in it, is yours so far as it can do you good. Even the enmity of the wicked will prove a blessing by disciplining you for heaven. If "ye are Christ's," "all things are yours." 1 Corinthians 3:23, 21.

But you are as a child who is not yet placed in control of his inheritance. God does not entrust to you your precious possession, lest Satan by his wily arts should beguile you, as he did the first pair in Eden. Christ holds it for you, safe beyond the spoiler's reach. Like the child, you shall receive day by day what is required for the day's need. Every day you are to pray, "Give us this day our daily bread." Be not dismayed if you have not sufficient for tomorrow. You have the assurance of His promise, "So shalt thou dwell in the land, and verily thou shalt be fed." David says, "I have been young, and now am old; yet have I not seen the righteous forsaken, nor his seed begging bread." Psalm 37:3, 25. That God who sent the ravens to feed Elijah by the brook Cherith will not pass by one of His faithful, self-sacrificing children. Of him that walketh righteously it is written: "Bread shall be given him; his waters shall be sure." "They shall not be ashamed in the evil time: and in the days of famine they shall be satisfied." "He that spared not His own Son, but delivered Him up for us all, how shall He not with Him also freely give us all things?" Isaiah 33:16; Psalm 37:19; Romans 8:32. He who lightened the cares and anxieties of His widowed mother and helped her to provide for the household at Nazareth, sympathizes with every mother in her struggle to provide her children food. He who had compassion on the multitude because they "fainted, and were scattered abroad" (Matthew 9:36), still has compassion on the suffering poor. His hand is stretched out toward them in blessing; and in the very prayer which He gave His disciples, He teaches us to remember the poor.

When we pray, "Give us this day our daily bread," we ask for others as well as ourselves. And we acknowledge that what God gives us is not for ourselves alone. God gives to us in trust, that we may feed the hungry. Of His goodness He has prepared for the poor. Psalm 68:10. And He says, "When thou makest a dinner or a supper, call not thy friends, nor thy brethren, neither thy kinsmen, nor thy rich neighbors.... But when thou makest a feast, call the poor, the maimed, the lame, the blind: and thou shalt be blessed; for they cannot recompense thee: for thou shalt be recompensed at the resurrection of the just." Luke 14:12-14.

"God is able to make all grace abound toward you; that ye, always having all sufficiency in all things, may abound to every good work." "He which soweth sparingly shall reap also sparingly; and he which soweth bountifully shall reap also bountifully." 2 Corinthians 9:8, 6.

The prayer for daily bread includes not only food to sustain the body, but that spiritual bread which will nourish the soul unto life everlasting. Jesus bids us, "Labor not for the meat which perisheth, but for that meat which endureth unto everlasting life." John 6:27. He says, "I am the living bread which came down from heaven: if any man eat of this bread, he shall live forever." Verse 51 . Our Saviour is the bread of life, and it is by beholding His love, by receiving it into the soul, that we feed upon the bread which came down from heaven.

[113] We receive Christ through His word, and the Holy Spirit is given to open the word of God to our understanding, and bring home its truths to our hearts. We are to pray day by day that as we read His word, God will send His Spirit to reveal to us the truth that will strengthen our souls for the day's need.

In teaching us to ask every day for what we need—both temporal and spiritual blessings—God has a purpose to accomplish for our good. He would have us realize our dependence upon His constant care, for He is seeking to draw us into communion with Himself. In this communion with Christ, through prayer and the study of the great and precious truths of His word, we shall as hungry souls be fed; as those that thirst, we shall be refreshed at the fountain of life.

"Forgive us our sins; for we also forgive everyone that is indebted to us."—Luke 11:4.

Jesus teaches that we can receive forgiveness from God only as we forgive others. It is the love of God that draws us unto Him, and that love cannot touch our hearts without creating love for our brethren.

After completing the Lord's Prayer, Jesus added: "If ye forgive men their trespasses, your heavenly Father will also forgive you: but if ye forgive not men their trespasses, neither will your Father forgive your trespasses." He who is unforgiving cuts off the very channel through which alone he can receive mercy from God. We should not think that unless those who have injured us confess the wrong we are justified in withholding from them our forgiveness. It is their part, no doubt, to humble their hearts by repentance and confession; but we are to have a spirit of compassion toward those who have trespassed against us, whether or not they confess their faults. However sorely they may have wounded us, we are not to cherish our grievances and sympathize with ourselves over our injuries; but as we hope to be pardoned for our offenses against God we are to pardon all who have done evil to us.

[114]

But forgiveness has a broader meaning than many suppose. When God gives the promise that He "will abundantly pardon," He adds, as if the meaning of that promise exceeded all that we could comprehend: "My thoughts are not your thoughts, neither are your ways My ways, saith the Lord. For as the heavens are higher than the earth, so are My ways higher than your ways, and My thoughts than your thoughts." Isaiah 55:7-9. God's forgiveness is not merely a judicial act by which He sets us free from condemnation. It is not only forgiveness *for* sin, but reclaiming *from* sin. It is the outflow of redeeming love that transforms the heart. David had the true conception of forgiveness when he prayed, "Create in me a clean heart, O God; and renew a right spirit within me." Psalm 51:10. And again he says, "As far as the east is from the west, so far hath He removed our transgressions from us." Psalm 103:12.

God in Christ gave Himself for our sins. He suffered the cruel death of the cross, bore for us the burden of guilt, "the just for the unjust," that He might reveal to us His love and draw us to Himself. And He says, "Be ye kind one to another, tenderhearted, forgiving each other, even as God also in Christ forgave you." Ephesians 4:32, R.V. Let Christ, the divine Life, dwell in you and through you reveal the heaven-born love that will inspire hope in the hopeless and bring heaven's peace to the sin-stricken heart. As we come to God, this is the condition which meets us at the threshold, that, receiving mercy from Him, we yield ourselves to reveal His grace to others.

[115]

The one thing essential for us in order that we may receive and impart the forgiving love of God is to know and believe the love that

He has to us. 1 John 4:16. Satan is working by every deception he can command, in order that we may not discern that love. He will lead us to think that our mistakes and transgressions have been so grievous that the Lord will not have respect unto our prayers and will not bless and save us. In ourselves we can see nothing but weakness, nothing to recommend us to God, and Satan tells us that it is of no use; we cannot remedy our defects of character. When we try to come to God, the enemy will whisper, It is of no use for you to pray; did not you do that evil thing? Have you not sinned against God and violated your own conscience? But we may tell the enemy that "the blood of Jesus Christ His Son cleanseth us from all sin." 1 John 1:7. When we feel that we have sinned and cannot pray, it is then the time to pray. Ashamed we may be and deeply humbled, but we must pray and believe. "This is a faithful saying, and worthy of all acceptation, that Christ Jesus came into the world to save sinners; of whom I am chief." 1 Timothy 1:15. Forgiveness, reconciliation with God, comes to us, not as a reward for our works, it is not bestowed because of the merit of sinful men, but it is a gift unto us, having in the spotless righteousness of Christ its foundation for bestowal.

We should not try to lessen our guilt by excusing sin. We must accept God's estimate of sin, and that is heavy indeed. Calvary alone can reveal the terrible enormity of sin. If we had to bear our own guilt, it would crush us. But the sinless One has taken our place; though undeserving, He has borne our iniquity. "If we confess our sins," God "is faithful and just to forgive us our sins, and to cleanse us from all unrighteousness." 1 John 1:9. Glorious truth!—just to His own law, and yet the Justifier of all that believe in Jesus. "Who is a God like unto Thee, that pardoneth iniquity, and passeth by the transgression of the remnant of His heritage? He retaineth not His anger forever, because He delighteth in mercy." Micah 7:18.

"Bring us not into temptation, but deliver us from the evil one."—Matthew 6:13, R. V.

Temptation is enticement to sin, and this does not proceed from God, but from Satan and from the evil of our own hearts. "God cannot be tempted with evil, and He Himself tempteth no man." James 1:13 , R.V.

Satan seeks to bring us into temptation, that the evil of our characters may be revealed before men and angels, that he may claim us as his own. In the symbolic prophecy of Zechariah, Satan is seen standing at the right hand of the Angel of the Lord, accusing Joshua, the high priest, who is clothed in filthy garments, and resisting the work that the Angel desires to do for him. This represents the attitude of Satan toward every soul whom Christ is seeking to draw unto Himself. The enemy leads us into sin, and then he accuses us before the heavenly universe as unworthy of the love of God. But "the Lord said unto Satan, The Lord rebuke thee, O Satan; even the Lord that hath chosen Jerusalem rebuke thee: is not this a brand plucked out of the fire?" And unto Joshua He said, "Behold, I have caused thine iniquity to pass from thee, and I will clothe thee with change of raiment." Zechariah 3:1-4.

God in His great love is seeking to develop in us the precious graces of His Spirit. He permits us to encounter obstacles, persecution, and hardships, not as a curse, but as the greatest blessing of our lives. Every temptation resisted, every trial bravely borne, gives us a new experience and advances us in the work of character building. The soul that through divine power resists temptation reveals to the world and to the heavenly universe the efficiency of the grace of Christ.

But while we are not to be dismayed by trial, bitter though it be, we should pray that God will not permit us to be brought where we shall be drawn away by the desires of our own evil hearts. In offering the prayer that Christ has given, we surrender ourselves to the guidance of God, asking Him to lead us in safe paths. We cannot offer this prayer in sincerity, and yet decide to walk in any way of our own choosing. We shall wait for His hand to lead us; we shall listen to His voice, saying, "This is the way, walk ye in it." Isaiah 30:21.

It is not safe for us to linger to contemplate the advantages to be reaped through yielding to Satan's suggestions. Sin means dishonor and disaster to every soul that indulges in it; but it is blinding and deceiving in its nature, and it will entice us with flattering presentations. If we venture on Satan's ground we have no assurance of protection from his power. So far as in us lies, we should close every avenue by which the tempter may find access to us.

The prayer, "Bring us not into temptation," is itself a promise. If we commit ourselves to God we have the assurance, He "will not suffer you to be tempted above that ye are able; but will with the temptation also make a way to escape, that ye may be able to bear it." 1 Corinthians 10:13.

The only safeguard against evil is the indwelling of Christ in the heart through faith in His righteousness. It is because selfishness exists in our hearts that temptation has power over us. But when we behold the great love of God, selfishness appears to us in its hideous and repulsive character, and we desire to have it expelled from the soul. As the Holy Spirit glorifies Christ, our hearts are softened and subdued, the temptation loses its power, and the grace of Christ transforms the character.

Christ will never abandon the soul for whom He has died. The soul may leave Him and be overwhelmed with temptation, but Christ can never turn from one for whom He has paid the ransom of His own life. Could our spiritual vision be quickened, we should see souls bowed under oppression and burdened with grief, pressed as a cart beneath sheaves and ready to die in discouragement. We should see angels flying swiftly to aid these tempted ones, who are standing as on the brink of a precipice. The angels from heaven force back the hosts of evil that encompass these souls, and guide them to plant their feet on the sure foundation. The battles waging between the two armies are as real as those fought by the armies of this world, and on the issue of the spiritual conflict eternal destinies depend.

To us, as to Peter, the word is spoken, "Satan hath desired to have you, that he may sift you as wheat: but I have prayed for thee, that thy faith fail not." Luke 22:31, 32. Thank God, we are not left alone. He who "so loved the world, that He gave His only-begotten Son, that whosoever believeth in Him should not perish, but have everlasting life" (John 3:16), will not desert us in the battle with the adversary of God and man. "Behold," He says, "I give unto you power to tread on serpents and scorpions, and over all the power of the enemy: and nothing shall by any means hurt you." Luke 10:19.

Live in contact with the living Christ, and He will hold you firmly by a hand that will never let go. Know and believe the love that God has to us, and you are secure; that love is a fortress impregnable to all the delusions and assaults of Satan. "The name of the Lord is a strong tower: the righteous runneth into it, and is safe." Proverbs 18:10.

"Thine is the kingdom, and the power, and the glory."—Matthew 6:13.

[120]

The last like the first sentence of the Lord's Prayer, points to our Father as above all power and authority and every name that is named. The Saviour beheld the years that stretched out before His disciples, not, as they had dreamed, lying in the sunshine of worldly prosperity and honor, but dark with the tempests of human hatred and satanic wrath. Amid national strife and ruin, the steps of the disciples would be beset with perils, and often their hearts would be oppressed by fear. They were to see Jerusalem a desolation, the temple swept away, its worship forever ended, and Israel scattered to all lands, like wrecks on a desert shore. Jesus said, "Ye shall hear of wars and rumors of wars." "Nation shall rise against nation, and kingdom against kingdom: and there shall be famines, and pestilences, and earthquakes, in divers places. All these are the beginning of sorrows." Matthew 24:6-8. Yet Christ's followers were not to fear that their hope was lost or that God had forsaken the earth. The power and the glory belong unto Him whose great purposes would still move on unthwarted toward their consummation. In the prayer that breathes their daily wants, the disciples of Christ were directed to look above all the power and dominion of evil, unto the Lord their God, whose kingdom ruleth over all and who is their Father and everlasting Friend.

The ruin of Jerusalem was a symbol of the final ruin that shall overwhelm the world. The prophecies that received a partial fulfillment in the overthrow of Jerusalem have a more direct application to the last days. We are now standing on the threshold of great and solemn events. A crisis is before us, such as the world has never witnessed. And sweetly to us, as to the first disciples, comes the assurance that God's kingdom ruleth over all. The program of coming events is in the hands of our Maker. The Majesty of heaven has the destiny of nations, as well as the concerns of His church, in His own charge. The divine Instructor is saying to every agent in the

[121]

accomplishment of His plans, as He said to Cyrus, "I girded thee, though thou hast not known Me." Isaiah 45:5.

In the vision of the prophet Ezekiel there was the appearance of a hand beneath the wings of the cherubim. This is to teach His servants that it is divine power which gives them success. Those whom God employs as His messengers are not to feel that His work is dependent upon them. Finite beings are not left to carry this burden of responsibility. He who slumbers not, who is continually at work for the accomplishment of His designs, will carry forward His own work. He will thwart the purposes of wicked men, and will bring to confusion the counsels of those who plot mischief against His people. He who is the King, the Lord of hosts, sitteth between the cherubim, and amid the strife and tumult of nations He guards His children still. He who ruleth in the heavens is our Saviour. He measures every trial, He watches the furnace fire that must test every soul. When the strongholds of kings shall be overthrown, when the arrows of wrath shall strike through the hearts of His enemies, His people will be safe in His hands.

[122]	"Thine, O Lord, is the greatness, and the power, and the glory, and the victory, and the majesty: for all that is in the heaven and in the earth is Thine.... In Thine hand is power and might; and in Thine hand it is to make great, and to give strength unto all." 1 Chronicles 29:11, 12.

Chapter 6—Not Judging, but Doing

"Judge not, that ye be not judged."—Matthew 7:1.

The effort to earn salvation by one's own works inevitably leads men to pile up human exactions as a barrier against sin. For, seeing that they fail to keep the law, they will devise rules and regulations of their own to force themselves to obey. All this turns the mind away from God to self. His love dies out of the heart, and with it perishes love for his fellow men. A system of human invention, with its multitudinous exactions, will lead its advocates to judge all who come short of the prescribed human standard. The atmosphere of selfish and narrow criticism stifles the noble and generous emotions, and causes men to become self-centered judges and petty spies.

The Pharisees were of this class. They came forth from their religious services, not humbled with a sense of their own weakness, not grateful for the great privileges that God had given them. They came forth filled with spiritual pride, and their theme was, "Myself, my feelings, my knowledge, my ways." Their own attainments became the standard by which they judged others. Putting on the robes of self-dignity, they mounted the judgment seat to criticize and condemn.

The people partook largely of the same spirit, intruding upon the province of conscience and judging one another in matters that lay between the soul and God. It was in reference to this spirit and practice that Jesus said, "Judge not, that ye be not judged." That is, do not set yourself up as a standard. Do not make your opinions, your views of duty, your interpretations of Scripture, a criterion for others and in your heart condemn them if they do not come up to your ideal. Do not criticize others, conjecturing as to their motives and passing judgment upon them.

"Judge nothing before the time, until the Lord come, who both will bring to light the hidden things of darkness, and will manifest the counsels of the hearts." 1 Corinthians 4:5. We cannot read the heart. Ourselves faulty, we are not qualified to sit in judgment upon others. Finite men can judge only from outward appearance. To Him alone who knows the secret springs of action, and who deals tenderly and compassionately, is it given to decide the case of every soul.

"Thou art inexcusable, O man, whosoever thou art that judgest: for wherein thou judgest another, thou condemnest thyself; for thou that judgest doest the same things." Romans 2:1. Thus those who condemn or criticize others, proclaim themselves guilty, for they do the same things. In condemning others, they are passing sentence upon themselves, and God declares that this sentence is just. He accepts their own verdict against themselves.

> "These clumsy feet, still in the mire,
> Go crushing blossoms without end;
> These hard, well-meaning hands we thrust
> Among the heartstrings of a friend."

[125] ## "Why beholdest thou the mote that is in thy brother's eye?"—Matthew 7:3.

Even the sentence, "Thou that judgest doest the same things," does not reach the magnitude of his sin who presumes to criticize and condemn his brother. Jesus said, "Why beholdest thou the mote that is in thy brother's eye, but considerest not the beam that is in thine own eye?"

His words describe one who is swift to discern a defect in others. When he thinks he has detected a flaw in the character or the life he is exceedingly zealous in trying to point it out; but Jesus declares that the very trait of character developed in doing this un-Christlike work, is, in comparison with the fault criticized, as a beam in proportion to a mote. It is one's own lack of the spirit of forbearance and love that leads him to make a world of an atom. Those who have never experienced the contrition of an entire surrender to Christ do not in their life make manifest the softening influence of the Saviour's love. They misrepresent the gentle, courteous spirit of the gospel and wound precious souls, for whom Christ died. According to the figure that our Saviour uses, he who indulges a censorious spirit is guilty of greater sin than is the one he accuses, for he not only commits the same sin, but adds to it conceit and censoriousness.

Christ is the only true standard of character, and he who sets himself up as a standard for others is putting himself in the place of Christ. And since the Father "hath committed all judgment unto the Son" (John 5:22), whoever presumes to judge the motives of others is again usurping the prerogative of the Son of God. These would-be judges and critics are placing themselves on the side of antichrist, "who opposeth and exalteth himself above all that is called God, or that is worshiped; so that he as God sitteth in the temple of God, showing himself that he is God." 2 Thessalonians 2:4.

The sin that leads to the most unhappy results is the cold, critical, unforgiving spirit that characterizes Pharisaism. When the religious experience is devoid of love, Jesus is not there; the sunshine of His presence is not there. No busy activity or Christless zeal can supply the lack. There may be a wonderful keenness of perception to discover the defects of others; but to everyone who indulges this spirit, Jesus says, "Thou hypocrite, first cast out the beam out of thine own eye; and then shalt thou see clearly to cast out the mote out of thy brother's eye." He who is guilty of wrong is the first to suspect wrong. By condemning another he is trying to conceal or excuse the evil of his own heart. It was through sin that men gained the knowledge of evil; no sooner had the first pair sinned than they began to accuse each other; and this is what human nature will inevitably do when uncontrolled by the grace of Christ.

When men indulge this accusing spirit, they are not satisfied with pointing out what they suppose to be a defect in their brother. If milder means fail of making him do what they think ought to be done, they will resort to compulsion. Just as far as lies in their power they will force men to comply with their ideas of what is right. This is what the Jews did in the days of Christ and what the church has done ever since whenever she has lost the grace of Christ. Finding herself destitute of the power of love, she has reached out for the strong arm of the state to enforce her dogmas and execute her decrees. Here is the secret of all religious laws that have ever been enacted, and the secret of all persecution from the days of Abel to our own time.

Christ does not drive but draws men unto Him. The only compulsion which He employs is the constraint of love. When the church begins to seek for the support of secular power, it is evident that she is devoid of the power of Christ—the constraint of divine love.

But the difficulty lies with the individual members of the church, and it is here that the cure must be wrought. Jesus bids the accuser first cast the beam out of his own eye, renounce his censorious spirit, confess and forsake his own sin, before trying to correct others. For "a good tree bringeth not forth corrupt fruit; neither doth a corrupt tree bring forth good fruit." Luke 6:43. This accusing spirit which you indulge is evil fruit, and shows that the tree is evil. It is useless for you to build yourselves up in self-righteousness. What you need is a change of heart. You must have this experience before you are fitted to correct others; for "out of the abundance of the heart the mouth speaketh." Matthew 12:34.

When a crisis comes in the life of any soul, and you attempt to give counsel or admonition, your words will have only the weight of influence for good that your own example and spirit have gained for you. You must *be* good before you can *do* good. You cannot exert an influence that will transform others until your own heart has been humbled and refined and made tender by the grace of Christ. When this change has been wrought in you, it will be as natural for you to live to bless others as it is for the rosebush to yield its fragrant bloom or the vine its purple clusters.

If Christ is in you "the hope of glory," you will have no disposition to watch others, to expose their errors. Instead of seeking to accuse and condemn, it will be your object to help, to bless, and to save. In dealing with those who are in error, you will heed the injunction, Consider "thyself, lest thou also be tempted." Galatians 6:1. You will call to mind the many times you have erred and how hard it was to find the right way when you had once left it. You will not push your brother into greater darkness, but with a heart full of pity will tell him of his danger.

He who looks often upon the cross of Calvary, remembering that his sins placed the Saviour there, will never try to estimate the degree of his guilt in comparison with that of others. He will not climb upon the judgment seat to bring accusation against another.

There can be no spirit of criticism or self-exaltation on the part of those who walk in the shadow of Calvary's cross.

Not until you feel that you could sacrifice your own self-dignity, and even lay down your life in order to save an erring brother, have you cast the beam out of your own eye so that you are prepared to help your brother. Then you can approach him and touch his heart. No one has ever been reclaimed from a wrong position by censure and reproach; but many have thus been driven from Christ and led to seal their hearts against conviction. A tender spirit, a gentle, winning deportment, may save the erring and hide a multitude of sins. The revelation of Christ in your own character will have a transforming power upon all with whom you come in contact. Let Christ be daily made manifest in you, and He will reveal through you the creative energy of His word—a gentle, persuasive, yet mighty influence to re-create other souls in the beauty of the Lord our God.

"Give not that which is holy unto the dogs."—Matthew 7:6.

Jesus here refers to a class who have no desire to escape from the slavery of sin. By indulgence in the corrupt and vile their natures have become so degraded that they cling to the evil and will not be separated from it. The servants of Christ should not allow themselves to be hindered by those who would make the gospel only a matter of contention and ridicule.

But the Saviour never passed by one soul, however sunken in sin, who was willing to receive the precious truths of heaven. To publicans and harlots His words were the beginning of a new life. Mary Magdalene, out of whom He cast seven devils, was the last at the Saviour's tomb and the first whom He greeted in the morning of His resurrection. It was Saul of Tarsus, one of the most determined enemies of the gospel, who became Paul the devoted minister of Christ. Beneath an appearance of hatred and contempt, even beneath crime and degradation, may be hidden a soul that the grace of Christ will rescue to shine as a jewel in the Redeemer's crown.

> "Ask, and it shall be given you; seek, and ye shall find; knock, and it shall be opened unto you."—Matthew 7:7.

To leave no chance for unbelief, misunderstanding, or misinterpretation of His words, the Lord repeats the thrice-given promise. He longs to have those who would seek after God believe in Him who is able to do all things. Therefore He adds, "For everyone that asketh receiveth; and he that seeketh findeth; and to him that knocketh it shall be opened."

The Lord specifies no conditions except that you hunger for His mercy, desire His counsel, and long for His love. "Ask." The asking, makes it manifest that you realize your necessity; and if you ask in faith you will receive. The Lord has pledged His word, and it cannot fail. If you come with true contrition you need not feel that you are presumptuous in asking for what the Lord has promised. When you ask for the blessings you need, that you may perfect a character after Christ's likeness, the Lord assures you that you are asking according to a promise that will be verified. That you feel and know you are a sinner is sufficient ground for asking for His mercy and compassion. The condition upon which you may come to God is not that you shall be holy, but that you desire Him to cleanse you from all sin and purify you from all iniquity. The argument that we may plead now and ever is our great need, our utterly helpless state, that makes Him and His redeeming power a necessity.

"Seek." Desire not merely His blessing, but Himself. "Acquaint now thyself with Him, and be at peace." Job 22:21. Seek, and you shall find. God is seeking you, and the very desire you feel to come to Him is but the drawing of His Spirit. Yield to that drawing. Christ is pleading the cause of the tempted, the erring, and the faithless. He is seeking to lift them into companionship with Himself. "If thou seek Him, He will be found of thee." 1 Chronicles 28:9.

"Knock." We come to God by special invitation, and He waits to welcome us to His audience chamber. The first disciples who followed Jesus were not satisfied with a hurried conversation with Him by the way; they said, "Rabbi, ... where dwellest Thou? ... They came and saw where He dwelt, and abode with Him that day." John 1:38, 39. So we may be admitted into closest intimacy and communion with God. "He that dwelleth in the secret place of the

Most High shall abide under the shadow of the Almighty." Psalm 91:1. Let those who desire the blessing of God knock and wait at the door of mercy with firm assurance, saying, For Thou, O Lord, hast said, "Everyone that asketh receiveth; and he that seeketh findeth; and to him that knocketh it shall be opened."

Jesus looked upon those who were assembled to hear His words, and earnestly desired that the great multitude might appreciate the mercy and loving-kindness of God. As an illustration of their need, and of God's willingness to give, He presents before them a hungry child asking his earthly parent for bread. "What man is there of *you*," He said, "whom if his son ask bread, will he give him a stone?" He appeals to the tender, natural affection of a parent for his child and then says, "If ye then, being evil, know how to give good gifts unto your children, how much more shall your Father which is in heaven give good things to them that ask Him?" No man with a father's heart would turn from his son who is hungry and is asking for bread. Would they think him capable of trifling with his child, of tantalizing him by raising his expectations only to disappoint him? Would he promise to give him good and nourishing food, and then give him a stone? And should anyone dishonor God by imagining that He would not respond to the appeals of His children?

If ye, then, being human and evil, "know how to give good gifts unto your children: how much more shall your heavenly Father give the Holy Spirit to them that ask Him?" Luke 11:13. The Holy Spirit, the representative of Himself, is the greatest of all gifts. All "good things" are comprised in this. The Creator Himself can give us nothing greater, nothing better. When we beseech the Lord to pity us in our distress, and to guide us by His Holy Spirit, He will never turn away our prayer. It is possible even for a parent to turn away from his hungry child, but God can never reject the cry of the needy and longing heart. With what wonderful tenderness He has described His love! To those who in days of darkness feel that God is unmindful of them, this is the message from the Father's heart: "Zion said, The Lord hath forsaken me, and my Lord hath forgotten me. Can a woman forget her sucking child, that she should not have compassion on the son of her womb? Yea, they may forget, yet will I not forget thee. Behold, I have graven thee upon the palms of My hands." Isaiah 49:14-16.

Every promise in the word of God furnishes us with subject matter for prayer, presenting the pledged word of Jehovah as our assurance. Whatever spiritual blessing we need, it is our privilege to claim through Jesus. We may tell the Lord, with the simplicity of a child, exactly what we need. We may state to Him our temporal matters, asking Him for bread and raiment as well as for the bread of life and the robe of Christ's righteousness. Your heavenly Father knows that you have need of all these things, and you are invited to ask Him concerning them. It is through the name of Jesus that every favor is received. God will honor that name, and will supply your necessities from the riches of His liberality.

But do not forget that in coming to God as a father you acknowledge your relation to Him as a child. You not only trust His goodness, but in all things yield to His will, knowing that His love is changeless. You give yourself to do His work. It was to those whom He had bidden to seek first the kingdom of God and His righteousness that Jesus gave the promise, "Ask, and ye shall receive." John 16:24.

The gifts of Him who has all power in heaven and earth are in store for the children of God. Gifts so precious that they come to us through the costly sacrifice of the Redeemer's blood; gifts that will satisfy the deepest craving of the heart, gifts lasting as eternity, will be received and enjoyed by all who will come to God as little children. Take God's promises as your own, plead them before Him as His own words, and you will receive fullness of joy.

"Therefore all things whatsoever ye would that men should do to you, do ye even so to them."—Matthew 7:12.

On the assurance of the love of God toward us, Jesus enjoins love to one another, in one comprehensive principle covering all the relations of human fellowship.

The Jews had been concerned about what they should receive; the burden of their anxiety was to secure what they thought their due of power and respect and service. But Christ teaches that our anxiety should not be, How much are we to receive? but, How much can we give? The standard of our obligation to others is found in what we ourselves would regard as their obligation to us.

In your association with others, put yourself in their place. Enter into their feelings, their difficulties, their disappointments, their joys, and their sorrows. Identify yourself with them, and then do to them as, were you to exchange places with them, you would wish them to deal with you. This is the true rule of honesty. It is another expression of the law. "Thou shalt love thy neighbor as thyself." Matthew 22:39. And it is the substance of the teaching of the prophets. It is a principle of heaven, and will be developed in all who are fitted for its holy companionship.

The golden rule is the principle of true courtesy, and its truest illustration is seen in the life and character of Jesus. Oh, what rays of softness and beauty shone forth in the daily life of our Saviour! What sweetness flowed from His very presence! The same spirit will be revealed in His children. Those with whom Christ dwells will be surrounded with a divine atmosphere. Their white robes of purity will be fragrant with perfume from the garden of the Lord. Their faces will reflect light from His, brightening the path for stumbling and weary feet.

No man who has the true ideal of what constitutes a perfect character will fail to manifest the sympathy and tenderness of Christ. The influence of grace is to soften the heart, to refine and purify the feelings, giving a heaven-born delicacy and sense of propriety.

But there is a yet deeper significance to the golden rule. Everyone who has been made a steward of the manifold grace of God is called upon to impart to souls in ignorance and darkness, even as, were he in their place, he would desire them to impart to him. The apostle Paul said, "I am debtor both to the Greeks, and to the barbarians; both to the wise, and to the unwise." Romans 1:14. By all that you have known of the love of God, by all that you have received of the rich gifts of His grace above the most benighted and degraded soul upon the earth are you in debt to that soul to impart these gifts unto him.

So also with the gifts and blessings of this life: whatever you may possess above your fellows places you in debt, to that degree, to all who are less favored. Have we wealth, or even the comforts of life, then we are under the most solemn obligation to care for the suffering sick, the widow, and the fatherless exactly as we would desire them to care for us were our condition and theirs to be reversed.

The golden rule teaches, by implication, the same truth which is taught elsewhere in the Sermon on the Mount, that "with what measure ye mete, it shall be measured to you again." That which we do to others, whether it be good or evil, will surely react upon ourselves, in blessing or in cursing. Whatever we give, we shall receive again. The earthly blessings which we impart to others may be, and often are, repaid in kind. What we give does, in time of need, often come back to us in fourfold measure in the coin of the realm. But, besides this, all gifts are repaid, even in this life, in the fuller inflowing of His love, which is the sum of all heaven's glory and its treasure. And evil imparted also returns again. Everyone who has been free to condemn or discourage, will in his own experience be brought over the ground where he has caused others to pass; he will feel what they have suffered because of his want of sympathy and tenderness.

It is the love of God toward us that has decreed this. He would lead us to abhor our own hardness of heart and to open our hearts to let Jesus abide in them. And thus, out of evil, good is brought, and what appeared a curse becomes a blessing.

The standard of the golden rule is the true standard of Christianity; anything short of it is a deception. A religion that leads men to place a low estimate upon human beings, whom Christ has esteemed of such value as to give Himself for them; a religion that would lead us to be careless of human needs, sufferings, or rights, is a spurious religion. In slighting the claims of the poor, the suffering, and the sinful, we are proving ourselves traitors to Christ. It is because men take upon themselves the name of Christ, while in life they deny His character, that Christianity has so little power in the world. The name of the Lord is blasphemed because of these things.

Of the apostolic church, in those bright days when the glory of the risen Christ shone upon them, it is written that no man said "that aught of the things which he possessed was his own." "Neither was there any among them that lacked." "And with great power gave the apostles witness of the resurrection of the Lord Jesus: and great grace was upon them all." "And they, continuing daily with one accord in the temple, and breaking bread from house to house, did eat their meat with gladness and singleness of heart, praising God, and having favor with all the people. And the Lord added to the church daily such as should be saved." Acts 4:32, 34, 33; 2:46, 47.

Search heaven and earth, and there is no truth revealed more powerful than that which is made manifest in works of mercy to those who need our sympathy and aid. This is the truth as it is in Jesus. When those who profess the name of Christ shall practice the principles of the golden rule, the same power will attend the gospel as in apostolic times.

"Strait is the gate, and narrow is the way, which leadeth unto life."—Matthew 7:14.

[138]

In the time of Christ the people of Palestine lived in walled towns, which were mostly situated upon hills or mountains. The gates, which were closed at sunset, were approached by steep, rocky roads, and the traveler journeying homeward at the close of the day often had to press his way in eager haste up the difficult ascent in order to reach the gate before nightfall. The loiterer was left without.

The narrow, upward road leading to home and rest furnished Jesus with an impressive figure of the Christian way. The path which I have set before you, He said, is narrow; the gate is difficult of entrance; for the golden rule excludes all pride and self-seeking. There is, indeed, a wider road; but its end is destruction. If you would climb the path of spiritual life, you must constantly ascend; for it is an upward way. You must go with the few; for the multitude will choose the downward path.

In the road to death the whole race may go, with all their worldliness, all their selfishness, all their pride, dishonesty, and moral debasement. There is room for every man's opinions and doctrines, space to follow his inclinations, to do whatever his self-love may dictate. In order to go in the path that leads to destruction, there is no need of searching for the way; for the gate is wide, and the way is broad, and the feet naturally turn into the path that ends in death.

But the way to life is narrow and the entrance strait. If you cling to any besetting sin you will find the way too narrow for you to enter. Your own ways, your own will, your evil habits and practices, must be given up if you would keep the way of the Lord. He who would serve Christ cannot follow the world's opinions or meet the world's

[139]

standard. Heaven's path is too narrow for rank and riches to ride in state, too narrow for the play of self-centered ambition, too steep and rugged for lovers of ease to climb. Toil, patience, self-sacrifice, reproach, poverty, the contradiction of sinners against Himself, was the portion of Christ, and it must be our portion, if we ever enter the Paradise of God.

Yet do not therefore conclude that the upward path is the hard and the downward road the easy way. All along the road that leads to death there are pains and penalties, there are sorrows and disappointments, there are warnings not to go on. God's love has made it hard for the heedless and headstrong to destroy themselves. It is true that Satan's path is made to appear attractive, but it is all a deception; in the way of evil there are bitter remorse and cankering care. We may think it pleasant to follow pride and worldly ambition, but the end is pain and sorrow. Selfish plans may present flattering promises and hold out the hope of enjoyment, but we shall find that our happiness is poisoned and our life embittered by hopes that center in self. In the downward road the gateway may be bright with flowers, but thorns are in the path. The light of hope which shines from its entrance fades into the darkness of despair, and the soul who follows that path descends into the shadows of unending night.

[140] "The way of transgressors is hard," but wisdom's "ways are ways of pleasantness and all her paths are peace." Proverbs 13:15; 3:17. Every act of obedience to Christ, every act of self-denial for His sake, every trial well endured, every victory gained over temptation, is a step in the march to the glory of final victory. If we take Christ for our guide, He will lead us safely. The veriest sinner need not miss his way. Not one trembling seeker need fail of walking in pure and holy light. Though the path is so narrow, so holy that sin cannot be tolerated therein, yet access has been secured for all, and not one doubting, trembling soul need say, "God cares nought for me."

The road may be rough and the ascent steep; there may be pitfalls upon the right hand and upon the left; we may have to endure toil in our journey; when weary, when longing for rest, we may have to toil on; when faint, we may have to fight; when discouraged, we must still hope; but with Christ as our guide we shall not fail of reaching the desired haven at last. Christ Himself has trodden the rough way before us and has smoothed the path for our feet.

And all the way up the steep road leading to eternal life are wellsprings of joy to refresh the weary. Those who walk in wisdom's ways are, even in tribulation, exceeding joyful; for He whom their soul loveth, walks, invisible, beside them. At each upward step they discern more distinctly the touch of His hand; at every step brighter gleamings of glory from the Unseen fall upon their path; and their songs of praise, reaching ever a higher note, ascend to join the songs of angels before the throne. "The path of the righteous is as the light of dawn, that shineth more and more unto the perfect day." Proverbs 4:18 , R.V., margin.

"Strive to enter in at the strait gate."—Luke 13:24.

The belated traveler, hurrying to reach the city gate by the going down of the sun, could not turn aside for any attractions by the way. His whole mind was bent on the one purpose of entering the gate. The same intensity of purpose, said Jesus, is required in the Christian life. I have opened to you the glory of character, which is the true glory of My kingdom. It offers you no promise of earthly dominion; yet it is worthy of your supreme desire and effort. I do not call you to battle for the supremacy of the world's great empire, but do not therefore conclude that there is no battle to be fought nor victories to be won. I bid you strive, agonize, to enter into My spiritual kingdom.

The Christian life is a battle and a march. But the victory to be gained is not won by human power. The field of conflict is the domain of the heart. The battle which we have to fight—the greatest battle that was ever fought by man—is the surrender of self to the will of God, the yielding of the heart to the sovereignty of love. The old nature, born of blood and of the will of the flesh, cannot inherit the kingdom of God. The hereditary tendencies, the former habits, must be given up.

He who determines to enter the spiritual kingdom will find that all the powers and passions of an unregenerate nature, backed by the forces of the kingdom of darkness, are arrayed against him. Selfishness and pride will make a stand against anything that would show them to be sinful. We cannot, of ourselves, conquer the evil desires and habits that strive for the mastery. We cannot overcome the mighty foe who holds us in his thrall. God alone can give us the victory. He desires us to have the mastery over ourselves, our own will and ways. But He cannot work in us without our consent and co-operation. The divine Spirit works through the faculties and powers given to man. Our energies are required to co-operate with God.

The victory is not won without much earnest prayer, without the humbling of self at every step. Our will is not to be forced into co-operation with divine agencies, but it must be voluntarily submitted. Were it possible to force upon you with a hundredfold greater intensity the influence of the Spirit of God, it would not make you a Christian, a fit subject for heaven. The stronghold of Satan would not be broken. The will must be placed on the side of God's will. You are not able, of yourself, to bring your purposes and desires and inclinations into submission to the will of God; but if you are "willing to be made willing," God will accomplish the work for you, even "casting down imaginations, and every high thing that exalteth itself against the knowledge of God, and bringing into captivity every thought to the obedience of Christ." 2 Corinthians 10:5. Then you will "work out your own salvation with fear and trembling. For it is God which worketh in you both to will and to do of His good pleasure." Philippians 2:12, 13.

But many are attracted by the beauty of Christ and the glory of heaven, who yet shrink from the conditions by which alone these can become their own. There are many in the broad way who are not fully satisfied with the path in which they walk. They long to break from the slavery of sin, and in their own strength they seek to make a stand against their sinful practices. They look toward the narrow way and the strait gate; but selfish pleasure, love of the world, pride, unsanctified ambition, place a barrier between them and the Saviour. To renounce their own will, their chosen objects of affection or pursuit, requires a sacrifice at which they hesitate and falter and turn back. Many "will seek to enter in, and shall not be able." Luke 13:24. They desire the good, they make some effort to obtain it; but they do not choose it; they have not a settled purpose to secure it at the cost of all things.

The only hope for us if we would overcome is to unite our will to God's will and work in co-operation with Him, hour by hour and day by day. We cannot retain self and yet enter the kingdom of God. If we ever attain unto holiness, it will be through the renunciation of self and the reception of the mind of Christ. Pride and self-sufficiency must be crucified. Are we willing to pay the price required of us? Are we willing to have our will brought into perfect conformity to the will of God? Until we are willing, the transforming grace of God cannot be manifest upon us.

The warfare which we are to wage is the "good fight of faith." "I also labor," said the apostle Paul, "striving according to His working, which worketh in me mightily." Colossians 1:29.

Jacob, in the great crisis of his life, turned aside to pray. He was filled with one overmastering purpose—to seek for transformation of character. But while he was pleading with God, an enemy, as he supposed, placed his hand upon him, and all night he wrestled for his life. But the purpose of his soul was not changed by peril of life itself. When his strength was nearly spent, the Angel put forth His divine power, and at His touch Jacob knew Him with whom he had been contending. Wounded and helpless, he fell upon the Saviour's breast, pleading for a blessing. He would not be turned aside nor cease his intercession, and Christ granted the petition of this helpless, penitent soul, according to His promise, "Let him take hold of My strength, that he may make peace with Me; and he shall make peace with Me." Isaiah 27:5. Jacob pleaded with determined spirit, "I will not let Thee go, except Thou bless me." Genesis 32:26. This spirit of persistence was inspired by Him who wrestled with the patriarch. It was He who gave him the victory, and He changed his name from Jacob to Israel, saying, "As a prince hast thou power with God and with men, and hast prevailed." Genesis 32:28. That for which Jacob had vainly wrestled in his own strength was won through self-surrender and steadfast faith. "This is the victory that overcometh the world, even our faith." 1 John 5:4.

"Beware of false prophets."—Matthew 7:15.

Teachers of falsehood will arise to draw you away from the narrow path and the strait gate. Beware of them; though concealed in sheep's clothing, inwardly they are ravening wolves. Jesus gives a test by which false teachers may be distinguished from the true. "Ye shall know them by their fruits," He says. "Do men gather grapes of thorns, or figs of thistles?"

We are not bidden to prove them by their fair speeches and exalted professions. They are to be judged by the word of God. "To the law and to the testimony: if they speak not according to this word it is because there is no light in them." "Cease, my son, to hear the instruction that causeth to err from the words of knowledge." Isaiah 8:20; Proverbs 19:27. What message do these teachers bring? Does it lead you to reverence and fear God? Does it lead you to manifest your love for Him by loyalty to His commandments? If men do not feel the weight of the moral law; if they make light of God's precepts; if they break one of the least of His commandments, and teach men so, they shall be of no esteem in the sight of heaven. We may know that their claims are without foundation. They are doing the very work that originated with the prince of darkness, the enemy of God.

Not all who profess His name and wear His badge are Christ's. Many who have taught in My name, said Jesus, will be found wanting at last. "Many will say to Me in that day, Lord, Lord, have we not prophesied in Thy name? and in Thy name have cast out devils? and in Thy name done many wonderful works? And then will I profess unto them, I never knew you: depart from Me, ye that work iniquity."

There are persons who believe that they are right, when they are wrong. While claiming Christ as their Lord, and professedly doing great works in His name, they are workers of iniquity. "With their mouth they show much love, but their heart goeth after their covetousness." He who declares God's word is to them "as a very lovely song of one that hath a pleasant voice, and can play well on an instrument: for they hear Thy words, but they do them not." Ezekiel 33:31, 32.

A mere profession of discipleship is of no value. The faith in Christ which saves the soul is not what it is represented to be by many. "Believe, believe," they say, "and you need not keep the law." But a belief that does not lead to obedience is presumption. The apostle John says, "He that saith, I know Him, and keepeth not His commandments, is a liar, and the truth is not in him." 1 John 2:4. Let none cherish the idea that special providences or miraculous manifestations are to be the proof of the genuineness of their work or of the ideas they advocate. When persons will speak lightly of the word of God, and set their impressions, feelings, and exercises above the divine standard, we may know that they have no light in them.

Obedience is the test of discipleship. It is the keeping of the commandments that proves the sincerity of our professions of love. When the doctrine we accept kills sin in the heart, purifies the soul from defilement, bears fruit unto holiness, we may know that it is the truth of God. When benevolence, kindness, tenderheartedness, sympathy, are manifest in our lives; when the joy of right doing is in our hearts; when we exalt Christ, and not self, we may know that our faith is of the right order. "Hereby we do know that we know Him, if we keep His commandments." 1 John 2:3.

"It fell not; for it was founded upon the rock."—Matthew 7:25, R. V.

The people had been deeply moved by the words of Christ. The divine beauty of the principles of truth attracted them; and Christ's solemn warnings had come to them as the voice of the heart-searching God. His words had struck at the very root of their former ideas and opinions; to obey His teaching would require a change in all their habits of thought and action. It would bring them into collision with their religious teachers; for it would involve the overthrow of the whole structure which for generations the rabbis had been rearing. Therefore, while the hearts of the people responded to His words, few were ready to accept them as the guide of life.

Jesus ended His teaching on the mount with an illustration that presented with startling vividness the importance of putting in practice the words He had spoken. Among the crowds that thronged about the Saviour were many who had spent their lives about the Sea of Galilee. As they sat upon the hillside, listening to the words of Christ, they could see valleys and ravines through which the mountain streams found their way to the sea. In summer these streams often wholly disappeared, leaving only a dry and dusty channel. But when the wintry storms burst upon the hills, the rivers became fierce, raging torrents, at times overspreading the valleys and bearing everything away on their resistless flood. Often, then, the hovels reared by the peasants on the grassy plain, apparently beyond the reach of danger, were swept away. But high upon the hills were houses built upon the rock. In some parts of the land were dwellings built wholly of rock, and many of them had withstood the tempests of a thousand years. These houses were reared with toil and difficulty. They were not easy of access, and their location appeared less inviting than the grassy plain. But they were founded upon the rock, and wind and flood and tempest beat upon them in vain.

Like the builders of these houses on the rock, said Jesus, is he who shall receive the words that I have spoken to you, and make them the foundation of his character and life. Centuries before, the prophet Isaiah had written, "The word of our God shall stand forever" (Isaiah 40:8); and Peter, long after the Sermon on the Mount was given, quoting these words of Isaiah added, "This is the word which by the gospel is preached unto you" (1 Peter 1:25). The word of God is the only steadfast thing our world knows. It is the sure foundation. "Heaven and earth shall pass away," said Jesus, "but My words shall not pass away." Matthew 24:35.

The great principles of the law, of the very nature of God, are embodied in the words of Christ on the mount. Whoever builds upon them is building upon Christ, the Rock of Ages. In receiving the word, we receive Christ. And only those who thus receive His words are building upon Him. "Other foundation can no man lay than that is laid, which is Jesus Christ." 1 Corinthians 3:11. "There is none other name under heaven, given among men, whereby we must be saved." Acts 4:12. Christ, the Word, the revelation of God,—the manifestation of His character, His law, His love, His life,—is the only foundation upon which we can build a character that will endure.

We build on Christ by obeying His word. It is not he who merely enjoys righteousness, that is righteous, but he who does righteousness. Holiness is not rapture; it is the result of surrendering all to God; it is doing the will of our heavenly Father. When the children of Israel were encamped on the borders of the Promised Land, it was not enough for them to have a knowledge of Canaan, or to sing the songs of Canaan. This alone would not bring them into possession of the vineyards and olive groves of the goodly land. They could make it theirs in truth only by occupation, by complying with the conditions, by exercising living faith in God, by appropriating His promises to themselves, while they obeyed His instruction.

Religion consists in doing the words of Christ; not doing to earn God's favor, but because, all undeserving, we have received the gift of His love. Christ places the salvation of man, not upon profession merely, but upon faith that is made manifest in works of righteousness. Doing, not saying merely, is expected of the followers of Christ. It is through action that character is built. "As many as are *led* by the Spirit of God, they are the sons of God." Romans 8:14. Not those whose hearts are touched by the Spirit, not those who now and then yield to its power, but they that are led by the Spirit, are the sons of God.

Do you desire to become a follower of Christ, yet know not how to begin? Are you in darkness and know not how to find the light? Follow the light you have. Set your heart to obey what you do know of the word of God. His power, His very life, dwells in His word. As you receive the word in faith, it will give you power to obey. As you give heed to the light you have, greater light will come. You are building on God's word, and your character will be builded after the similitude of the character of Christ.

Christ, the true foundation, is a living stone; His life is imparted to all that are built upon Him. "Ye also, as living stones, are built up a spiritual house." "Each several building, fitly framed together, groweth into a holy temple in the Lord." 1 Peter 2:5 , R.V.; Ephesians 2:21 , R.V. The stones became one with the foundation; for a common life dwells in all. That building no tempest can overthrow; for—

> "That which shares the life of God,
> With Him surviveth all."

But every building erected on other foundation than God's word will fall. He who, like the Jews in Christ's day, builds on the foundation of human ideas and opinions, of forms and ceremonies of man's invention, or on any works that he can do independently of the grace of Christ, is erecting his structure of character upon the

[151] shifting sand. The fierce tempests of temptation will sweep away the sandy foundation and leave his house a wreck on the shores of time.

"Therefore thus saith the Lord God, ... Judgment also will I lay to the line, and righteousness to the plummet: and the hail shall sweep away the refuge of lies, and the waters shall overflow the hiding place." Isaiah 28:16, 17.

But today mercy pleads with the sinner. "As I live, saith the Lord God, I have no pleasure in the death of the wicked; but that the wicked turn from his way and live: turn ye, turn ye from your evil ways; for why will ye die?" Ezekiel 33:11. The voice that speaks to the impenitent today is the voice of Him who in heart anguish exclaimed as He beheld the city of His love: "O Jerusalem, Jerusalem, which killeth the prophets, and stoneth them that are sent unto her! how often would I have gathered thy children together, even as a hen gathereth her own brood under her wings, and ye would not! Behold, your house is left unto you desolate." Luke 13:34, 35, R.V. In Jerusalem, Jesus beheld a symbol of the world that had rejected and despised His grace. He was weeping, O stubborn heart, for you! Even when Jesus' tears were shed upon the mount, Jerusalem might yet have repented, and escaped her doom. For a little space the Gift of heaven still waited her acceptance. So, O heart, to you Christ is still speaking in accents of love: "Behold, I stand at the door, and knock: if any man hear My voice, and open the door, I will come in to him, and will sup with him, and he with Me." "Now is the accepted time; behold, now is the day of salvation." Revelation 3:20; 2 Corinthians 6:2.

[152] You who are resting your hope on self are building on the sand. But it is not yet too late to escape the impending ruin. Before the tempest breaks, flee to the sure foundation. "Thus saith the Lord God, Behold, I lay in Zion for a foundation a stone, a tried stone, a precious cornerstone, of sure foundation: he that believeth shall not make haste." "Look unto Me, and be ye saved, all the ends of the earth: for I am God, and there is none else." "Fear thou not; for I am with thee: be not dismayed; for I am thy God: I will strengthen thee; yea, I will help thee; yea, I will uphold thee with the right hand of My righteousness." "Ye shall not be ashamed nor confounded world without end." Isaiah 28:16, R.V.; 45:22; 41:10; 45:17.

www.ingramcontent.com/pod-product-compliance
Lightning Source LLC
Chambersburg PA
CBHW080859010526
44118CB00015B/2205